ANNULMENT

ANNULMENT
100 QUESTIONS
AND ANSWERS
FOR CATHOLICS

Pete Vere & Jacqui Rapp

SERVANT
BOOKS

PUBLISHED BY ST. ANTHONY MESSENGER PRESS
CINCINNATI, OHIO

RESCRIPT

In accord with the *Code of Canon Law,* I hereby grant my permission to publish *Annulment: 100 Questions and Answers for Catholics.*

Reverend Joseph R. Binzer
Vicar General
Archdiocese of Cincinnati
Cincinnati, Ohio
October 6, 2009

Permission to Publish is a declaration that a book or pamphlet is considered to be free of doctrinal or moral error. It is not implied that those who have granted the Permission to Publish agree with the contents, opinions or statements expressed.

Unless otherwise noted, Scripture passages have been taken from the *Revised Standard Version,* Catholic edition. Copyright 1946, 1952, 1971 by the Division of Christian Education of the National Council of Churches of Christ in the USA. Used by permission. All rights reserved.

Note: The editors of this volume have made minor changes in capitalization to some of the Scripture quotations herein. Please consult the original source for proper capitalization.

Cover design by Candle Light Studios
Cover image copyright by Shutterstock
Book design by Mark Sullivan

LIBRARY OF CONGRESS CATALOGING-IN-PUBLICATION DATA
Vere, Pete.
Annulment : 100 questions and answers for Catholics / Pete Vere and Jacqueline Rapp.
   p. cm.
Includes bibliographical references and index.
ISBN 978-0-86716-873-0 (pbk. : alk. paper) 1. Marriage—Religious aspects—Catholic Church—Miscellanea. 2. Marriage—Annulment—Miscellanea. I. Rapp, Jacqueline. II. Title.
BX2250.V47 2009
262.9'47—dc22

2009029806

ISBN 978-0-86716-873-0

Published by Servant Books, an imprint of St. Anthony Messenger Press.
28 W. Liberty St.
Cincinnati, OH 45202
www.ServantBooks.org

Printed in the United States of America.

Printed on acid-free paper.

09 10 11 12 13 5 4 3 2 1

contents

acknowledgments

Thanks to my mentors and friends through the years as a canonist: Dr. John Huels, Michel Theriault, Monsignor Jace Eskind (who got me through comprehensives), Archbishop Thomas C. Kelly, O.P. (who had the faith to give me my first job), Very Reverend J. Mark Spalding, Reverend Philip Erickson and Amy Jill Strickland.

Thanks to Cindy Cavnar for her guidance and sanity.

Thanks to my friend, co-conspirator and godmother to my babies, Trish Hansen, who convinced me that I could write a book. In particular, thanks to my husband and best friend, Keith, for the love and nudging needed to complete this book, and to my daughters, Alex and Sabina, for the inspiration to be the best I can be.

—Jacqui Rapp

I would first like to thank my wife, Sonya, for watching the kids at various KOA and Jellystone campgrounds in northern Michigan while I completed this book.

I also wish to thank my professors at St. Paul University, especially Father William Woestman, Father Frank Morrisey, Father Gus Mendonca, Dr. John Huels and Lynda Robitaille; as well as former classmate Michael Trueman, who encouraged me to go forward with this project and always made himself available for advice.

A big thank you to Monsignor Pat Pratico, Joe Fox and Linda Price for giving me my first tribunal job with the diocese of Scranton; as well as Father Joe Amato and Father John Dolciamore at the diocese of Venice in Florida, who imparted their decades of tribunal experience while I was serving as their defender of the bond. From my local diocese in Sault Ste. Marie, I wish to thank Bishop Jean-Louis Plouffe, Father Bob Bourgon, Rosemary Cappadocia and Linda Labelle.

A special thank-you to my students and fellow faculty at Catholic Distance University (CDU.edu), for asking many of the questions that inspired this book.

Another special thank-you goes out to Corporal James Wells and the staff at the Canadian Forces Chaplaincy School. Having served his country faithfully for decades as a frontline soldier, Corporal Wells now serves the next generation of soldiers by ensuring that incoming military chaplains receive the support, training and equipment they need.

I also wish to thank Cindy Cavnar, Lucy Scholand and Chris Holmes from Servant Books for their hard work, dedication and professionalism in bringing together this book project.

Most importantly, I thank Saint Joseph, foster father of our Lord, without whose intercession I would not be practicing my Catholic faith.

—*Pete Vere*

introduction

Isn't an annulment just a Catholic divorce? Do I need to hire a lawyer? If the Church annuls my marriage, do my children become illegitimate? These are some of the many questions laypeople struggle with when contemplating an annulment.

The decision to pursue an annulment is extremely personal, and so is the process. The individual will be asked to revisit his or her former relationship, from the first date to the divorce, to discover why the marriage broke down.

Actually the term *annulment* is a misnomer, however since it is what most people call the process, this book will continue to use the term. As you will discover in reading this book, the Church does not annul marriages; she declares them invalid. What this means is that a Church court, when sufficient evidence is presented, declares that from the beginning something important was missing from a relationship. This "something important" is essential to every marriage, whether the vows were exchanged between baptized Catholics or between two nonbaptized pagans on a tropical island. Thus the absence of this "something important" prevented the union from becoming a marriage as understood by Church teaching.

But more on this later.

As canon lawyers with over fifteen years of Church tribunal experience between us, the authors understand how intimidating this process can appear when first being considered. The purpose of this book is to ease your fears, answer your concerns and help you increase your understanding of what's going on. By breaking down the legal jargon and applying it to particular situations in a question-and-answer format, we hope to make your reading easy, even when the subject matter is difficult.

Breaking with other books written for laity on annulments, we have ventured into some related canonical areas. For instance, you'll find a chapter on marriage preparation and another on how the Church defines marriage. Should you find yourself in a position to marry within the Church, you will have a better understanding of how the Church defines this relationship and what is required to enter it.

So take your time, enjoy the read and expand your knowledge about canon law, marriage and why the Church declares some marriages invalid.

chapter one

General Questions About Annulments

1. Will my children become illegitimate if the Church declares my former marriage invalid?

This is by far the most common question asked about the annulment process. It is also the source of the most misunderstandings among laity, as well as some clergy and religious. Even before Catholics ask themselves what is meant by the expression "declaration of invalidity" or how the process for declaring a marriage invalid functions, they want to know how an annulment will affect their children's status within the Church.

The answer is that it won't. The Church is very clear that children of a "putative marriage" are considered legitimate. A putative marriage is one that was entered into in good faith by at least one party but later was judged by the Church to be invalid. Thus the annulment process judges the validity of the marriage and not of the children born of the marriage.

This teaching is found in canon 1137 of the *Code of Canon Law,* a book that includes most of the laws, or canons, to which the Latin Catholic Church adheres when judging annulment cases. (Eastern Catholic Churches have their own code of canon law.) In short, the Church recognizes that we sometimes make mistakes. Children are never a mistake. They may be unexpected or come at a difficult time, but God loves them, and so do their parents. Thus the Church would not have children punished because something was lacking in their parents' marriage.

2. So what is a "declaration of invalidity," commonly referred to as an "annulment" or a "declaration of nullity"?

A declaration of invalidity is a statement of fact issued by the Catholic Church. After carefully examining a couple's broken relationship, the Church states that a marriage, as the Church defines marriage, never truly existed between them. The relationship may have enjoyed some of the external trappings of marriage: There may have been a big wedding followed by a common address and the birth of children. However, not all weddings bring about a marriage.

When something essential to marriage is lacking in a relationship from the very beginning—and don't worry about that "something" right now, as we'll deal with this in the following chapters—the Church may declare a marriage invalid. Of course, an exhaustive investigation is required in most instances, since the Church is judging whether an important human relationship actually happened.

Thus, the commonly used word *annulment* is somewhat misleading. The Church does not annul a marriage—that is, cancel it or end it. Rather, the Church declares that an obstacle prevented the relationship from coming together as a marriage. The issue had to be serious, and it had to be present at the time of the wedding.

3. How much do declarations of invalidity cost? Is it true that only rich people can afford to have the Church look at their case?

There is no cost for a declaration of invalidity. After all, the Catholic faithful have a right to know their sacramental status within the Church. Everyone, Catholic and non-Catholic, has the opportunity provided to them to have their prior marriages investigated. But there are fees for the process whereby the Church investigates the alleged invalidity.

The cost of processing an annulment case varies from diocese to diocese. As this book is being written—in the year 2009—the cost to an American diocese is roughly $2,000. This takes into account personnel, supplies and all of the things that are necessary to keep an average office working. Few dioceses charge the full amount. Most ask for some sort of fee, to be paid by the petitioner, to offset the total costs. This fee can range anywhere from a few dollars to several hundred dollars.

Rome has made it very clear that the inability to pay should not determine whether a person is able to have a case heard. Therefore all dioceses offer some sort of fee reduction to those who show financial need. The rest of the money for the process may come from the financial appeal made by each diocese on a yearly basis.

Clearly the idea that only the rich can receive a declaration of invalidity, or that your chances of receiving such a declaration depend upon your financial contributions to the diocese, is a misconception.

4. Is it true that you "have to know someone" to get an annulment?
Often people are of the belief that you must "know the right people" in order to receive a declaration of invalidity. Nothing could be further from the truth. In fact, knowing someone in

the tribunal can make things more challenging for you and the tribunal in question. Judges are prohibited from hearing cases in which they may have a personal interest. This includes cases involving relatives, guardianship, intimate acquaintances (because of common life, business partnership or very close friendship), hostile relationships or a possible financial loss or gain (see canon 1448).

This prohibition also applies to other tribunal personnel, such as the defender of the bond, who represents the marriage bond in a case; assessor, which is a fancy word for an individual brought in to help judges evaluate evidence; and auditors, who record the testimonies of the parties. Therefore there are fewer complications in cases where the person knows nobody at the tribunal than where the person has "connections."

5. Does a declaration of invalidity have any effect in civil law? And will I need to hire my own lawyer to represent me at the tribunal?

Here in North America the answer to both questions is no. Because Canada and the United States maintain a strict separation between church and state, a declaration of invalidity has no effects in civil law. Consequently civil authorities feel no need to get involved in the process, which affects only one's status within the Church.

Similarly, there is generally no need to hire one's own canon lawyer in North America. Most parishes have at least one priest or deacon who is trained to begin the declaration of invalidity process. Once the tribunal takes over, the parties may be given a list of canonical advocates (see question 63) approved by the diocese. In difficult cases the tribunal may appoint a canon lawyer as advocate for someone to ensure that his or her rights are defended within the process. However, this process differs from diocese to diocese; not every diocesan tribunal automatically appoints advocates for the parties.

The parties nevertheless are free to hire their own canon lawyers from outside the diocese. In such a circumstance the canon lawyer must seek approval from the diocese before representing the party. The canon lawyer must also deposit a mandate with the tribunal, that is, a signed statement from the party establishing that he or she is being represented by the canon lawyer.

The situation is different in parts of the world where a declaration of invalidity by a Church tribunal is recognized by the civil courts or substitutes for a divorce decree by a civil court. The Church may be asked to oversee the division of assets, custody of children, alimony and child support. In these geographical regions it is prudent to hire a canon lawyer.

6. You keep using the word tribunal. What is a tribunal anyway, and how does it apply to my declaration of invalidity?

A tribunal is a Church court. Each diocese is required by canon law—that is, the Church's internal legal system—to have a tribunal. The diocesan bishop appoints the tribunal's personnel, ensuring that each individual has the proper credentials and qualifications for the office. The bishop also appoints a judicial vicar to oversee the tribunal on his behalf. The judicial vicar decides which cases to accept and which personnel to assign to particular cases.

Diocesan tribunals function much as do secular courts. A case must be introduced in the form of a complaint, and various legal procedures must be followed during each stage of the process. The tribunal personnel are similar to those one would find in a secular court. For instance, a case is overseen by a sole judge or a college of three judges. A party to the case may obtain the services of an advocate, who acts as legal counsel. Auditors collect evidence on behalf of the judge, often fleshing out answers and asking further questions to help the judge better understand the evidence. Each tribunal appoints ecclesiastical notaries, who attest to the authenticity of individual court documents. Chapter six discusses each of the tribunal personnel in more detail.

Throughout the process, parties and their advocates are given the opportunity to introduce evidence, question the evidence of opposing parties and present their arguments. The tribunal judges hear all the evidence, both for and against the validity of the marriage, and then make a decision.

7. *You have also mentioned the term* canon law. *What is canon law, and how does it differ from civil law or criminal law?*

Every organization, whether secular or religious, requires its own laws and customs in order to maintain order. The internal legal system that governs the day-to-day workings of the Catholic Church is known as canon law. It functions much like civil law in that it deals with a wide variety of topics that touch upon our daily lives, providing ways of avoiding problems and offering equitable solutions when problems do arise.

The word *canon* comes from the old Greek word *kanon*, which means "reed." In the ancient world a reed symbolized the authority to rule.

There are two Latin words for *law*: *lex* and *ius*. *Lex* refers to an individual or particular law. From its plural form *leges* we derive the English words *legislator* and *legislation*. The term *ius*, on the other hand, means an entire system of law or the subject of law in the abstract. From it we derive the English words *justice* and *jurisprudence*. When the Church employs the term *canon law*, it is referring to *ius*. Thus the *Code of Canon Law*–which contains most of the Church's basic laws (*leges*)– is known in Latin as the *Codex Iuris Canonici*.

Canon law differs from civil law in North America and most English-speaking countries in that it has no effect outside of the Church, unless secular courts choose to recognize it as a form of personal law. Canon law also follows the principles of Roman law, which sometimes differ from the Anglo-American common law tradition followed by the civil courts. For example, under canon law a precedent set by a higher tribunal does not necessarily bind lower tribunals.

8. What if my former spouse and I had children? Is it true that the Church grants declarations of invalidity only when no children were born of the marriage?

The lack of children can help prove certain grounds for declaring a marriage invalid. For example, if refusal to have children is the reason for questioning the marriage's validity, then the lack of children could provide evidence of the refusal's firmness. Yet the presence of children does not necessarily mean that a marriage is valid.

Remember that the Church judges the state of the parties when they exchanged their wedding vows. A person can possess enough physical maturity to conceive children while lacking the psychological and emotional maturity necessary to undertake the responsibilities of marriage. For example, an alcoholic who cannot hold down a job, squanders the family budget on his addiction and physically abuses his wife and children when withdrawing from alcohol is incapable of living up to his responsibilities as husband and father. (Something his spouse does not discover until after the wedding.) The subsequent birth of children would not validate his marriage if at the time of the wedding his alcoholism prevented him from assuming the responsibilities of husband and potential father.

In fact, the birth of children into a relationship will often reveal the cause for a declaration of invalidity. Using the previous example, a wife might tolerate an alcoholic husband's violent outbursts and financial irresponsibility early on in the relationship but lose patience when the behavior continues after the birth of a child. After all, who wants to expose young children to alcoholism and abuse? Or the problem might worsen after a child is born. Some "social" drinkers can become daily drinkers to try to cope with the stress of raising a newborn.

Regardless, the birth of children does not validate an invalid marriage.

9. *Whom should I contact to begin an investigation into my former marriage?*

While every tribunal must follow the same procedures once a case is underway, each diocese is unique when it comes to getting a case off the ground. Sometimes the method differs among parishes within the same diocese.

For example, some dioceses require the petitioner—that is, the person seeking the declaration of nullity—to approach the diocesan tribunal directly. Other dioceses delegate the parish priest as the point of initial contact for the petitioner. A diocese may also train individual deacons, religious and laity to help petitioners begin the tribunal process. Or, if a diocese covers a large geographical area and is broken down into regions, a person or parish from each region may serve as the initial contact point for the petitioner.

Regardless of how your local diocese has set this up, it is best to approach your parish priest first. He can then list the options available to you, provide other pastoral care and if necessary refer the case to another qualified individual. Chapter seven answers questions about the annulment process in more detail.

10. I am not Catholic, and I was previously married to another non-Catholic before a non-Catholic minister. Why must I go through the tribunal process if my previous marriage had nothing to do with the Catholic Church?

If you are not Catholic but plan to marry a Catholic, you might be asked to go through the annulment process. This seems odd to most non-Catholics when neither person from the first union is Catholic. Why should the Catholic Church investigate this marriage?

The Catholic Church presumes the validity of any marriage between two people who are free to marry at the time of their wedding (canon 1060). To be free to marry, either a person must have no previous marriages, or the spouse from any previous marriage must be deceased. Because God instituted marriage in the Old Testament, long before Christ raised it to the dignity of a sacrament, marriage belongs to all people and not only Catholics.

The Church recognizes any marriage between two non-Catholics who are free to marry, so long as civil society and the religious community to which either spouse belongs recognize the wedding as valid. It does not matter whether the marriage takes place before a Protestant minister, a rabbi, or an imam, or before a civil official. And since marriage, as God created it, is permanent, the Church must investigate the prior marriages of any non-Catholics seeking to marry in the Church.

chapter two

The Meaning of Marriage

11. What does the Church mean by marriage? Why is this important to the declaration of invalidity process?

We'll answer the second part of your question first.

When a Church tribunal declares a marriage invalid, the Church is saying that the marriage never existed. Therefore it is important that the Church have a strong understanding of marriage. After all, how can the Church declare something to have not taken place if it does not know what that something is?

To define marriage within this context, canon lawyers—that is, those approved by the Church to work within diocesan tribunals—turn to the *Code of Canon Law.* The code is broken down into canons (individual laws), of which canon 1055 describes marriage as a covenant between one man and one woman. (Thus, right away the Church excludes polygamous, polyandrous and same-sex unions from her understanding of marriage.) The couple establish the marital covenant for life. The purpose of this covenant is to provide for the well-being of the spouses as well as for the conception, birth and upbringing of children.

The aforementioned is common to all valid marriages, including those between Catholics, non-Catholic Christians and those who are not Christian. When a marriage between two nonbaptized individuals or between one baptized and one non-baptized meets this standard, canon lawyers refer to the union as a "natural marriage." This means the marriage follows the teaching of natural law—that is, the law of nature that God has written in every human heart.

An example of a natural marriage is one between a Jewish couple. The same is true of a marriage between a Mormon couple, because the Church does not recognize the validity of Mormon baptism.

When a marriage is entered into by two baptized people, Christ raises the covenant to the dignity of a sacrament. This means husband and wife become for each other a source of God's grace. Every valid marriage between two baptized Christians is a sacramental marriage—regardless of whether one or both spouses are Catholic.

12. What is a covenant within the context of marriage?
The idea of covenant in the Bible is one of a strong pact between humans or between God and humans. Within this pact each party promises to assist the other toward a common goal. For example, in the Old Testament a covenant exists between God and the people of Israel. This special relationship is sealed for eternity.

In marriage the covenant is between a man and a woman. The spouses establish this covenant through their marital consent, commonly exchanged in their wedding vows. Through these vows both husband and wife express their intention to establish between themselves a partnership for the whole of life. This means each spouse will assist and support the other in all areas of their new life together, the best he or she is able, so long as the other spouse is alive. They will support each other emotionally, physically, financially, socially and in the raising of their children.

Within a sacramental marriage, spouses will also support each other spiritually. In other words, husband and wife will help each other deepen their relationship with God and the Church. Thus, like other sacraments, the couple's marriage becomes a source of God's sanctifying grace.

13. Did the Church always understand marriage as a covenant? Why do old Catholic textbooks refer to it as a contract?

Prior to the Second Vatican Council, the Church emphasized marriage not as a covenant but primarily as a *contract*. (To provide some historical background, the Church, at least in the West, borrowed the language of *contract* from the ancient Roman legal system.) In practice this meant that so long as each individual was free to marry, intended to contract a marriage, stood before a priest and exchanged wedding vows, they were married. The bride and groom were bound to the marital contract regardless of the purpose for which they entered into it.

Come the 1983 *Code of Canon Law,* the Church firmly introduced the language of *covenant* into its legal understanding of marriage. The word *covenant* is quite pronounced in the opening of canon 1055. Similarly, the 1990 *Code of Canons of the Eastern Churches* (*CCEO*), which governs Eastern Catholics, stresses the language of *covenant*. In fact, the first paragraph of *CCEO* canon 776 defines marriage as a covenant established by the Creator. The rest of the canon parallels what is written in canon 1055 of the *Code of Canon Law*. Thus the Church's covenantal understanding of marriage is a relatively new—but firm—development.

14. What is the difference between a contract and a covenant?

A covenant gives rise to a much deeper relationship than does a contract. Intrinsic to a covenant is the welfare of the other person, who in this case is the intended spouse.

Let us borrow an example from a canon lawyer in the middle ages who found the whole concept of contract problematic when applied to the sacrament of marriage. In discussing his concerns, he proposed the following hypothetical situation to his students:

There are two feuding families—one has a son, and one has a daughter. Let's Anglicize this example and name these young people Romeo and Juliet. One day Romeo concocts a plan through which he intends to get back at Juliet and her family. He decides to court her until she accepts his marriage proposal, at which point he will "stand in the right place and say the right things." He promises Juliet fidelity, lots of children and a lifelong marriage. In short, he enters into marriage with the intention to fulfill all the contractual obligations required by the Church. Yet Romeo also intends to make this marriage abusive for Juliet—belittling her and hitting her at the slightest provocation—in order to avenge his family in their feud against her family.

Is this truly a marriage, as the Church ought to understand this sacrament? The canon law professor did not believe so, and neither did many of his students. Yet at the time he proposed this hypothetical situation, many canonists did.

Romeo met and fulfilled all the contractual obligations of his wedding vows. He intended to remain faithful so long as both he and Juliet lived, and he fully intended to bring children into the relationship. Under the contractual model of marriage, this would be a highly abusive marriage but nevertheless a valid one.

This does not hold, however, when we understand marriage as a covenant. After all, when the mutual welfare of the spouses enters into the Church's understanding of marriage, how can the relationship between Romeo and Juliet rise to the level of marriage? As previously mentioned, not every wedding brings about a marriage.

15. What are the two elements of marriage? Why are they important to the Church's understanding of marriage?

The goal of the marriage covenant, by its very nature, is the mutual welfare of the spouses (physical, emotional and spiritual) as well as openness to the procreation, welfare and education of children. This is what makes marriage a unique relationship: Husband and wife promise to place the welfare of each other before their own. Additionally, each spouse promises to be open to a sexual relationship that is open to the possibility of children and to assist the other in looking after the welfare of any children born of the marriage.

Without these two common purposes, marriage would be little more than a business partnership. Thus the Church refers to the good of the spouses and the good of children as the two elements of marriage. All genuine marriages, whether Christian or non-Christian, must contain these two elements. They are natural to marriage.

The Church bases this natural understanding of marriage on the text of Genesis 2:18–25, which teaches that God's will has established all marriages. True marriage is heterosexual (between a man and a woman); it is monogamous (between one man and one woman); it is exclusive (the two form a new and unique relationship, becoming one); and it is permanent (if the two become one, this new union cannot be divided, a conclusion Christ confirms in Matthew 19:3–12).

16. What does the first element, the mutual welfare of the spouses, entail?

Genesis 2:18–25 states that God created all the animals and brought them before Adam to be named. But a "suitable partner" was not found for him among them. So God created the woman, and Adam responded: "This at last is bone of my bones / and flesh of my flesh" (verse 23).

This passage confirms what the Church teaches about marriage: that it involves partners who are suitable for each other through the sharing of strengths and weaknesses. When Adam says, "Bone of my bones," he is saying, "This one is strong where I am strong." And when he says, "Flesh of my flesh," he is saying, "This one is weak where I am weak." Thus the marriage covenant is ordered toward the mutual welfare of the spouses, in that the couple share their strengths and their weaknesses as they work together for their common good as husband and wife.

Of course, no marriage is perfect. Like any other human relationship, every marriage has its ups and downs. However, the Church expects spouses to work through their differences, forgive each other when they have been less than patient with one another and give the relationship their best effort.

17. What does the second element, the good of children, entail?

The connection between marriage and children is established in the opening chapter of Genesis, where God tells Adam and Eve to "be fruitful and multiply" (Genesis 1:28). Thus, marriage is also about "fruitfulness" or bringing children into the world and raising them to maturity (procreation and education).

By education the Church means not only the academic education of children but their social, moral, religious and cultural education as well. In short, by its very nature marriage requires a couple to raise any children brought into the world as a result of the marital covenant.

An interesting question arises when a couple are incapable of bearing children through no fault of their own. Is their marriage still recognized by the Church? The answer is yes, provided the couple were open to the procreation and education of children when they contracted the marriage. In such cases the couple's inability to conceive is beyond their control, and they must simply accept it as God's will. Of course, such couples may also consider adoption.

18. Why does the Church speak of marriage as a partnership of life and love? Aren't wives supposed to be subject to their husbands?

Another important development in canon law since the Second Vatican Council is the recognition of marriage as a partnership. When taken with the good of the spouses, marriage is understood as a communion of life and love. This understanding comes directly from Holy Scripture.

Saint Paul states in his Letter to the Ephesians:

Wives, be subject to your husbands, as to the Lord. For the husband is the head of the wife as Christ is the head of the Church, his body, and is himself its Savior. As the

Church is subject to Christ, so let wives also be subject in everything to their husbands. (Ephesians 5:22–24)

In the past this Scripture passage has been misinterpreted to excuse everything from domestic violence to the subjugation of women within the institution of marriage.

Yet within the context of Saint Paul's writings, this passage touches upon the matrimonial theology of partnership, mutual welfare of the spouses and a covenant of life and love. The verse prefacing this passage is clear: "Be subject to one another out of reverence for Christ" (Ephesians 5:21). As is the passage that comes afterward:

Husbands, love your wives, as Christ loved the Church and gave himself up for her.... Even so husbands should love their wives as their own bodies. He who loves his wife loves himself. For no man ever hates his own flesh, but nourishes and cherishes it, as Christ does the Church. (Ephesians 5:25, 28–29)

In short, the marital partnership is implicit in Saint Paul's injunction that husbands and wives be subject to one another out of reverence for Christ. Similarly, communion of life and love is implied within this passage. Saint Paul teaches that a husband's love, to which a wife subjects herself, should be a self-sacrificing reflection of how Christ loves the Church. For just as Christ laid down his life for the Church out of a deep love for us, so, too, should a husband lay down his life for his wife if love requires it.

Obviously, such a tremendous love rules out domestic violence, belittling and other forms of marital abuse, for one should never abuse and belittle one's own flesh.

19. What are the two properties of marriage? Do they differ from the two elements of marriage?

In addition to the two elements, by its nature marriage possesses what canon lawyers call the two properties of marriage. We call them the two properties because they belong to every marriage, regardless of whether it is natural or sacramental. These properties are unity and permanence.

In noncanonical parlance these properties are more commonly known by their respective derivatives, namely, fidelity and permanence. Like the two elements of marriage, the properties are common to every true marriage, regardless of whether the marriage is between Christians or non-Christians.

These properties are essential to marriage. This means they belong to marriage in such a way that marriage cannot exist without them. Thus the Church does not recognize polygamous unions, since these lack unity. Similarly the Church does not recognize temporary or trial marriages, since these lack permanence.

20. What is the property of unity common to every marriage?

When canon lawyers speak of the unity of marriage, we refer to the fact that husband and wife enter into a unique relationship to the exclusion of all others. As we read in Holy Scripture, "Therefore a man leaves his father and his mother and clings to his wife, and they become one flesh" (Genesis 2:24). Thus the relationship between a husband and a wife should be even stronger than the relationship between a child and a parent. After all, marriage is a spiritual bond, whereas the parent-child relationship is a natural bond.

Fidelity is a key ingredient of the unitive property within marriage. In pledging fidelity to one another while exchanging their wedding vows, a couple exclude any sexual relationship with a third party. This lays a foundation of trust through which the couple establish a communion of life and love. Because marriage is ordered toward the good of children and the mutual welfare of the spouses, a husband must be able to trust his wife and vice versa. He feels secure knowing his wife's children are also his, and she feels secure knowing her husband's exclusive focus is on caring for her and helping her raise their children.

21. What is the property of indissolubility common to every marriage?

Indissolubility, the second property of marriage, means the couple bind themselves to their wedding vows until they are separated by death. This is an important property of marriage because it concerns the stability of the relationship between husband and wife. To form a partnership of life and love, each party must be capable of trusting that the other will always be committed to the relationship. Regardless of what difficulties arise during the course of the marriage, a person knows his or her spouse will share the burdens.

Thus indissolubility derives from the perpetual property of marriage. In the case of a sacramental marriage—that is, a marriage between two baptized Christians—only God may dissolve the marriage. He does so through the death of one of the spouses.

The Church may dissolve a non-sacramental marriage while both of the spouses are still alive. Yet because permanence remains the ideal, the Church may dissolve a non-sacramental marriage only when certain exceptional circumstances arise. We will discuss these circumstances in more detail in chapter three, but one of the circumstances in some cases should be noted here: The Church must first ascertain that the petitioning party was not responsible for the breakup of the marriage.

22. What about sacramentality? How does this fit in with the Church's theology of marriage?

Sacramentality is a third property of marriage. Unlike unity and permanence, however, sacramentality is not common to every marriage.

When husband and wife are baptized Christians, their marriage becomes a sacrament, that is, a visible sign of God's love in the world. This means that the couple find in their relationship a source of God's grace, and through their partnership they assist one another in coming closer to God.

Sacramentality happens automatically when both spouses are validly baptized. This includes marriages between two validly baptized non-Catholics, even though many Protestants do not believe that marriage is a sacrament. It does not matter where two baptized Protestants married or who performed the ceremony. The sacramentality of their marriage depends completely upon the baptismal status of the man and the woman.

Baptism is the gateway to all of the other sacraments, and thus both spouses must be baptized for their union to take on the property of sacramentality. A marriage between a baptized person and a nonbaptized person is a natural marriage, not a sacramental one.

When a marriage is sacramental, the properties of marriage take on a special firmness. As a sacrament the marriage becomes a source of sanctifying grace, which strengthens the bond of unity. Likewise the property of permanence is stronger because the couple's bond is spiritual and not just natural, and thus only God can dissolve it.

23. Can a natural marriage become a sacramental marriage if the nonbaptized spouse or spouses receive baptism during the marriage?

Yes, a natural marriage takes on sacramentality if both of the parties become baptized at any point during the marriage. For example, if two nonbaptized atheists marry, and several years later both convert to Catholicism and receive baptism, their marriage becomes a sacrament at that point.

Similarly, if a baptized individual marries a nonbaptized individual, and the nonbaptized spouse subsequently receives baptism during the course of the marriage, the natural marriage is raised to a sacramental one. This takes place upon the baptism of the previously non-baptized spouse. The Church considers it impossible for two baptized people to be married without their marriage being a sacrament.

Nevertheless, a marriage between two nonbaptized people does not take on the property of sacramentality when only one spouse subsequently receives baptism. As noted in the previous question, marriage is a union between two people. Therefore both spouses must be baptized for their marriage to take on sacramentality.

24. When does marriage come into being?

Marriage comes into being through lawfully manifested

consent—that is, there must be a taking of the other as spouse in a way recognizable to the community to which the parties belong. When two people give themselves to one another in order to create a partnership of life and love, and they do so in a manner recognized by the community, they marry. For two nonbaptized people this can happen in front of a justice of the peace in the middle of a field. Baptized Christians can marry wherever their faith community recognizes the marriage.

Canon law differs between Eastern and non-Eastern Catholics. Among Eastern Catholics, the blessing of a priest or bishop is required for validity. Catholics must communicate marital consent during the wedding ceremony. The presider must ask for and receive the consent of the man and the woman. This is normally done through the exchange of wedding vows.

25. *What is the canonical form of marriage? Are Catholics required to follow it?*

When at least one of the parties is Catholic, the Church requires the parties to express their desire to give themselves in marriage before a priest, a deacon or a designated witness, (this last possibility is rare in North America) with two other witnesses. The priest or qualified witness must request the exchange of consent for the marriage to be valid. This is known as the canonical form of marriage.

If a Catholic desires to enter marriage with a non-Catholic outside of this form, a dispensation may be granted. This is a relaxation of the law requiring the Catholic party to follow canonical form. The dispensation allows the parties to exchange their consent in another manner. Nevertheless, this kind of dispensation is an exception rather than the rule.

The canonical form of marriage arose in response to several abuses throughout the Church's history. During the Middle Ages an errant knight might seduce a maiden by exchanging wedding vows in private, then deny his actions the next morning—breaking the young woman's heart. Or upon discovering she was pregnant by the town drunk, an unscrupulous maiden might say she had exchanged vows in private with an innocent knight, because of his higher social status. The knight would then be forced to clear his name. You can imagine the chaos caused by the private exchange of wedding vows within medieval society. Thus the Church imposed the canonical form, requiring all wedding vows to be exchanged publicly before the parish priest.

This requirement, however, led to the problem of "surprise marriages." An eager young couple would see a priest strolling in public, approach him unexpectedly and exchange their wedding vows before he could object. Because the couple had expressed their consent publicly before a priest, the Church considered surprise marriages valid. So the Church added a further requirement to the canonical form, namely that the priest must request the consent of the parties for the marriage to be valid.

chapter three

Marriage Preparation in Canon Law

26. How are pastors supposed to prepare couples for marriage?
The Church talks of remote, proximate and immediate preparation for marriage.

Remote preparation is that which takes place throughout a person's life: It begins with one's experiences growing up in a family. Other remote preparation takes place in school, in formation groups and in society at large. Canon law obliges pastors to ensure that each person receives the assistance he or she needs in order to enter marriage fruitfully (canon 1063). Pastors are to use preaching, catechesis and other methods of communication to instruct the Catholic faithful about the meaning of Christian marriage and the functions of spouses and parents.

Proximate preparation begins when a couple decide to marry. Normally this occurs during marriage preparation courses offered within the diocese or the parish, by people who are solidly formed in Church teaching on marriage and family.

The document "Preparation for the Sacrament of Marriage," created by the Pontifical Council for the Family, offers some guidance. The document states that proximate preparation should include information about God's plan for marriage and family, about marital consent and those things that could hinder valid marital consent, about permanence and the exclusivity of marriage, about the Church's teachings on responsible parenthood and about sexuality and the right of each party to a relationship that is open to the procreation and education of children. You will notice that we cover many of these issues in this book.

Immediate preparation takes place in the final months before the wedding. The couple review all they have learned and receive the appropriate spiritual and liturgical preparation for the actual wedding and the marriage. According to canon 1063, pastors must assist the couple in this preparation, ensuring a "fruitful liturgical celebration of marriage which is to show that the spouses signify and share in the mystery of the unity and fruitful love between Christ and the Church." This is usually done in the context of marriage preparation programs, such as Engaged Encounter, or with trained couples in the parish. Jacqui and her husband, Keith, are trained to help their parish priest prepare couples for the sacrament of marriage.

Marriage preparation does not end with the wedding. Canon law envisions the pastor helping the couple in the early stages of their marriage and beyond to lead a holy and fulfilled marriage and family life.

27. What should we do if our marriage preparation program seemed out of touch with current issues facing couples today? What if the course presented ideas at odds with Church teaching?

The second question arose during Pete's premarital preparation course with his wife (then fiancée), Sonya. The instructors asked each couple to share what form of contraception they would use during their marriage. When Pete and Sonya declined to answer the question, the instructors confronted them in front of the other engaged couples. Citing their background in moral theology and quoting some dissenting theologians on the issue, the instructors told Pete and Sonya that the Church had changed its teaching on contraception.

Pete informed the instructors that he was just finishing his license in canon law, and that the Church most certainly had *not* changed its teaching contained in *Humanae Vitae*. Sonya, a biologist, then added scientific information on the negative effects of contraception on a woman's health. Later Pete and Sonya complained to the diocesan chancellor, who had come by to bless the engaged couples. The chancellor promised to address the problem in future courses.

Canon law is clear that the bishop is responsible for ensuring appropriate marriage preparation be available in his diocese (canon 1064). Canon law also instructs the Christian faithful to make known their spiritual needs and desires to the Church's pastors. This is both a right and an obligation of canon law (canon 212, paragraph 2). Therefore, if a couple believe that their marriage preparation program did not fully prepare them for what they will face as a married couple, living out marriage as the Church teaches, then those parties should approach their pastor. He can then approach the local family ministries office of the diocese or the individual in charge of marriage preparation programs. The couple should follow the same course of action if they believe their premarital program presents ideas contrary to orthodox Catholic teaching.

If they were to feel so inclined, the couple could also contact the family ministries office and share their concerns. Pete and Sonya's discussion with the chancellor was in keeping with that directive.

Obviously, every program should be revised with time. A marriage preparation program written in the 1960s may not be appropriate for couples entering marriage in 2010. The best way for those who run these programs to be sure that the appropriate messages are being sent to the couples is to hear from the couples themselves.

28. Do you have to be confirmed to marry in the Church?

This is one of those great myths that have taken root in the minds of many Catholics—that one cannot marry in the Church unless one first receives confirmation. Yes, the Church encourages every Catholic to receive confirmation prior to marriage, so that spouses may benefit from additional sacramental grace as they undertake their new relationship together. However, confirmation is not an absolute prerequisite to Catholic marriage.

According to canon 1065, confirmation should be conferred on a party to be married if it can be done "without grave inconvenience." A person should never be rushed into receiving a sacrament (canon 843, paragraph 2). If proper preparation for confirmation cannot be realized, then the Church does not wish to push it. Baptism is the sacrament that determines whether the marriage is a sacrament, not confirmation.

29. Must the couple go to confession before marrying?

Much like confirmation, the sacrament of reconciliation is

not required prior to entering into marriage. If the parties do not go to confession, the validity of the marriage is not affected. Having said that, one always should enter into a sacrament with the proper disposition to receive it (canon 843, paragraph 1).

Canon 1065 urges the future husband and wife to receive the sacrament of reconciliation and partake of the Most Holy Eucharist prior to their wedding vows, so that the couple can receive the sacrament of marriage fruitfully. The ideal situation for marriage is that it bring together two people of faith who want to do what the Church teaches and who want to have a full experience of the sacrament.

30. What is with all of this marriage paperwork?

There seems to be a lot of paperwork prior to getting married. There's the paperwork at the city hall, or wherever you go to get a marriage license, and then there are all the contracts that must be signed with various wedding vendors. However, the paperwork that you go through with the Church has serious meaning.

Canon 1066 requires that, prior to the wedding, it is clearly established that nothing prevents the couple from lawfully marrying in the Church. So the question becomes, how does the Church investigate a person's freedom to marry?

A long time ago, when people lived most of their lives within the same community (and communities were much smaller than today's metropolises), banns were published. For several Sundays in a row, the couple would stand up after Mass while the priest announced their intent to marry. If anyone knew of anything that stood in the way of the couple's lawful marriage, they were to come forward and notify the priest.

The publication of banns is no longer a common practice. Given how mobile society has become, and how large our communities have grown, banns are no longer an efficient way of establishing the parties' freedom to marry. Hence the paperwork, through which the pastor or premarital investigator asks various questions of the couple. Their answers help the pastor discern whether anything prevents the couple from marrying within the Church, such as a prior marriage that ended in divorce or some underlying psychological issue with one or both of the parties. Or perhaps one of the parties is too young.

These procedures can be altered in situations in which one or both parties is in danger of death, either intrinsically (that is, through grave illness) or extrinsically (in time of war or natural disaster, for example), per canon 1068.

31. What should a person do if he or she knows something that prevents a couple from validly marrying in the Church?

Canon 1069 requires the Christian faithful to make known to their pastors or local ordinaries any impediments to marriage prior to a wedding. The canon is quite strict concerning this responsibility, using the word *obliged*. Thus it is clear that someone in this situation must report the impediment to the pastor, episcopal vicar, vicar general or diocesan bishop. The responsibility then falls upon the competent Church authority to investigate the situation and handle it appropriately.

This canon takes into account the fact that sometimes people are incapable of revealing information they know. For example, a priest hearing the sacramental confession of a bride-to-be discovers that she is underage. Or a professional psychologist learns about a person's psychological impediment in the course of professional therapy. Because these types of relationships do not allow a person to share what he or she knows, it is important that others in the community come forward if need be. Similarly, it is important that the couple be open and honest when questioned by their pastor.

32. If a couple live in a state other than the one in which they're marrying, how does the pastor know that they have completed their marriage preparation?

In the best of all possible worlds, the pastor prepares the couple for marriage. However, this is sometimes impractical given the demands placed on the time of most pastors—especially when couples live in communities other than the one in which they wish to marry. Perhaps the bride-to-be went out of state for college, where she met the love of her life. Or perhaps the groom-to-be found work out of town and is now coming home to wed his high school sweetheart and carry her off into the sunrise. ("Sunset" would sound rather ominous in a book about broken marriages.)

For reasons such as these, a pastor can entrust the marriage preparation of couples, as well as the investigation into whether the parties are free to marry, to other qualified people. Canon 1070 requires that the person entrusted with the premarital investigation notify the pastor of the findings as soon as possible. A document must be signed, dated and sealed with the parish seal of the premarital investigator (canon 535, paragraph 3). This way the pastor can rest assured that the proper investigation and preparation have been made, preferably well before the wedding is scheduled.

There is nothing worse than a pastor finding out the day of the wedding that an impediment prevents the couple from lawfully marrying, all because the pastor learns something he should have been told about months before. Pete has encountered this problem while working in tribunal ministry. Although tribunal staff rushed to complete the proper paperwork at the last moment, this was not always possible. Consequently families found themselves justifiably angry and couples disappointed—especially when they had poured thousands of dollars into the wedding, and friends and family had booked vacations around it.

33. Do certain types of marriage require the bishop's approval before they can proceed?

Yes. In fact, there are several different situations for which the bishop must give his permission before the wedding can proceed in the Catholic Church. However, these scenarios affect the wedding's lawfulness only and not its validity. In other words, the Church still considers the couple married if they proceed without the bishop's permission.

The scenarios are outlined in canon 1071 as follows:

1. A marriage involving a transient or wanderer (someone with no fixed address, making it difficult to prove anything about him or her and carry out the proper premarital investigations)

2. A marriage that cannot be recognized or celebrated by civil law (for example, a marriage between interracial

couples during apartheid in South Africa or in certain U.S. states prior to the Civil Rights Movement)

3. A marriage of a person bound by previous marital or parental obligations (that is, obligations to prior spouses or children, be they emotional, financial or whatever)

4. A marriage of someone who has notoriously rejected the Catholic faith (someone who is professing something contrary to the Catholic faith)

5. A marriage of a person under censure (a penalty under canon law—specifically excommunication and interdict; if you're under this penalty, you'll know it!)

6. A marriage involving a minor (anyone under the age of eighteen, per canon 97, paragraph 1) when the parents are either unaware or opposed

7. A marriage entered into by proxy (where one party—or both—is not present and is represented by another person)

These are all delicate pastoral situations that require special pastoral care. Hence the need to obtain the bishop's permission, due to his obligation to care for the spiritual needs of his community. Moreover, the bishop would be forced to defend the marriage should news of the wedding become public in his diocese.

34. Does this mean I need the bishop's permission to marry someone who has stopped practicing the Catholic faith?

No. Canon 1071 is not referring to those who are merely lax in the practice of their Catholic faith. To reject the faith is much more serious than not to practice it any longer, or to practice it only on Christmas and Easter. To reject the faith means to choose intentionally to practice an idea or religion contrary to the Catholic faith.

Proving notorious rejection can be a difficult task. For example, a Catholic who checks out the local Baptist service has probably not rejected his or her Catholic faith. On the other hand, accepting rebaptism in the local Baptist chapel or receiving ordination to Baptist ministry would be a clear indication of rejecting one's Catholic faith.

This type of situation is a serious drawback for the party still practicing the Catholic faith—especially as it affects children born into the marriage. The Church has grave concerns that the practicing Catholic remain a practicing Catholic after the wedding, and that he or she do all within his or her power to raise the children Catholic. Therefore, just as for any other mixed-marriage couple, the Catholic party must promise to do all that he or she can to remain a practicing Catholic and raise any children in the Catholic faith (see canon 1125).

35. My fiancé and I are currently living together. Can we still get married in the Church?

Just because two people live in the same space does not mean that they are sexually active outside the covenant of marriage. Some couples choose to live in the same space to save money. This does not make the situation right; however, the Church teaches that people should refrain from presumptions that the couple are "living in sin." Priests, deacons and laity are to avoid rash judgments about cohabiting couples and are therefore to interpret the couple's thoughts, words and deeds in a favorable way.

That being said, people are also to avoid situations that

could lead to sin. Living with someone, as if married, often leads to a false sense of intimacy. This increases the temptation to fall into an inappropriate sexual relationship.

Priests, of course, are concerned with the salvation of the souls of those who approach them for the sacraments. They must also protect the dignity of the sacraments, thus being concerned about those who attempt to partake of the sacraments without being properly disposed. It is of the greatest importance that cohabiting couples avail themselves of the sacrament of reconciliation prior to the wedding (preferably earlier that day).

To answer the question as originally posed, there is no impediment in the *Code of Canon Law* prohibiting those who cohabit prior to marriage from celebrating marriage. All those who have a wedding liturgy have the right to a liturgical celebration that is valid, worthy and fruitful (*Familiaris Consortio* 67; canon 1063, 3). Note that the wedding is called a "celebration," and every couple has the right to a true celebration of their covenant.

chapter four

Impediments to Marriage

36. *What is an impediment?*

An impediment is a fact or condition that disqualifies a person from validly entering into a marriage. The word *impediment* is used because the individual is "impeded" from contracting marriage in the Catholic Church.

When the impediment is well-known or can be proven publicly, canon lawyers refer to it as public. For example, it would be obvious that a man and a woman born of the same mother and raised in the same household are brother and sister. Their marriage is impeded by their close blood relationship, which canon lawyers refer to as *consanguinity*.

On the other hand, an impediment is considered *occult* when it is not known by most people or cannot be proven publicly. *Occult* in this context does not refer to Harry Potter, witches or pagan rituals summoning the devil (or a giant purple dinosaur). Rather it is an old Latin word meaning *hidden*.

For instance, suppose a man and a woman are twins born out of wedlock to a teenage mother. Let's call the twins Luke and Leia. The birth mother gives her twins up to a Catholic adoption agency shortly after birth, which in turn adopts them out to different families. The records are then sealed to protect the privacy of the birth mother.

Luke and Leia meet in college, discover they were both adopted and share the same birthday, and enjoy a mutual passion for astronomy, laser technology and Olympic fencing. The starry-eyed couple then fall in love without realizing they are brother and sister. While the impediment of blood is not known to Luke or Leia, it is nevertheless present. The occult impediment would prevent the couple from marrying validly.

An impediment is either *relative* or *absolute*. It is relative when it disqualifies someone from marrying a specific person. Consanguinity is an example of a relative impediment (no pun intended): Brother and sister cannot marry each other, but each may marry someone else, provided there are no other impediments. On the other hand, an impediment is absolute when it prohibits a person from marrying *any* other person.

37. How are impediments established or recognized by canon lawyers?

Impediments arise from one of two sources. The first is natural law, that is, the law of nature written by God on the hearts of men. A good example of such is certain degrees of consanguinity, or blood relation.

Leviticus 18:6 validates this: "None of you shall approach any one near of kin to him to uncover nakedness." Subsequent verses identify various degrees of next of kin that are prohibited from sexual intercourse with each other. The natural law impediments identified in subsequent passages include relations between parent and child, siblings and half-siblings.

The Church may also establish impediments to marriage for other reasons, besides those found in the natural law, such as for individuals ordained to the clerical state or those consecrated as religious (that is, sisters and brothers). Only the Holy See can establish a permanent impediment.

38. Can an impediment be removed or overcome if it is not temporary?

The answer depends upon the impediment in question. In some cases the Church may dispense diriment impediments, that is, relax the law in order to permit the marriage to go forward. However, the Church cannot dispense an impediment based upon natural law. This is because God's law is higher than mere Church law. Thus consanguinity in the direct line (parent and child, grandparent and grandchild and so on) or consanguinity in the second degree collateral (brother and sister, half-brother and half-sister) are not open to dispensation.

Canon 1078 allows the local ordinary to dispense from an impediment that is based solely on Church law, provided the impediment is not reserved to the Holy See. An impediment "reserved to the Holy See" can only be dispensed by the Holy Father or one delegated by him. The impediments reserved to the Holy See are crime, holy orders and public perpetual vows in an institute of consecrated life of pontifical right.

39. What is the impediment of crime?

The impediment of crime is murder—not just any murder but the murder of a spouse with the intent of entering into another marriage. The reason for this impediment is twofold. First, it protects the sanctity of life and marriage. Second, it prevents someone from benefitting from the murder of his or her spouse.

The impediment of crime can apply in one of three ways.

• The first is when one murders one's own spouse to attempt marriage with another party. Let's use the example of Adam and Eve as the married couple and Steve as the third party. If Eve falls in love with Steve at an office party, she cannot murder Adam in order to marry Steve without incurring the impediment of crime. Should she murder Adam anyway, her subsequent marriage to Steve would be invalid. However, she could marry someone other than Steve validly, since her original intention in murdering Adam was to marry Steve.

• The impediment of crime also arises when an individual murders the spouse of someone whom he or she wishes to marry. Thus Steve could not murder Adam without incurring the impediment of crime with Eve. This is true even if Eve were ignorant of Steve's involvement in Adam's death. However, because the impediment of crime is relative, Steve could marry a woman other than Eve.

• The third way in which this impediment applies is when two people cooperate in the death of a spouse, even though there is no intention to marry at the time. Suppose Steve is a hit man. Eve hires Steve because she wants to collect Adam's life insurance. Even though Eve and Steve have no intention of marrying each other once Adam is murdered, the impediment of crime arises should Eve and Steve subsequently fall in love. But again the impediment is relative. Thus nothing—except possibly prison—would prevent Eve and Steve from marrying other people.

40. What about the impediment of holy orders and public perpetual vows?

The impediment of holy orders is ordination. If a man is ordained a deacon, a priest or a bishop, he is impeded from validly entering into marriage. This impediment arises from the obligation of celibacy. The Holy See may dispense from this impediment when a cleric has requested dispensation from the clerical state.

In the case of permanent deacons, the Holy See will sometimes dispense from this impediment and allow the deacon to marry and continue in ministry if certain conditions are present.

As for public perpetual vows in religious institutes, admittedly this is quite a mouthful. This impediment applies to clergy, religious brothers and religious sisters who have professed their vows publicly and in perpetuity. Thus the impediment does not apply to novices and others who have professed only temporary vows.

41. What if the impeded individual is dying and there isn't enough time to approach the Holy See? Is there some other means of dispensing from an impediment reserved to the Holy See?

Yes. Canon 1079 allows the local ordinary to dispense from an impediment reserved to the Holy See when one of the parties requesting the marriage is in danger of death. The only exceptions are impediments that arise from ordination to the presbyterate. Thus a bishop, vicar general or episcopal vicar could dispense a deacon but not a priest from the impediment of holy orders or a religious brother or sister from the impediment of public perpetual vows; the same Church authorities could dispense a layperson from the impediment of crime.

The canon applies regardless of whether the impediment is public or occult. The canon also applies regardless of whether the person in danger of death is the impeded individual or the intended spouse.

If the local ordinary cannot be reached in time, the same canon allows the officiant to dispense from an impediment normally reserved to the Holy See. The same conditions apply as for the local ordinary. The canon even specifies that a local ordinary who can be reached only through telegraph or telephone (and, one can presume, e-mail) is not considered accessible according to canon law.

42. What are some of the more common impediments listed in the Code of Canon Law?

Fortunately, crime is a very rare impediment in North American society today. The code lists several other impediments that are much more common: Three of these are age, impotence and prior bond.

The impediment of age applies to males who have not completed their sixteenth year and females who have not completed their fourteenth year. Because marriage is a lifelong decision, the Church wishes to ensure that a couple possess sufficient maturity before undertaking such a relationship. Therefore a man must be at least sixteen years of age before he can validly enter into a marriage, and a woman at least fourteen.

Canon 1083 allows a conference of bishops to set a higher age for their territory. However, this does not affect the validity of the marriage. Should a sixteen-year-old man and a fourteen-year-old woman wed without meeting their episcopal conference's higher age requirements, the Church would still consider their marriage valid.

The impediment of impotence arises when a person is physically or psychologically unable to engage in sexual intercourse. Impotence may be absolute, which means the person is unable to engage in sexual intercourse with anyone; it is relative when the person is incapable of engaging in intercourse only with the person he or she attempts to marry. Impotence is not the same thing as sterility—the latter being the incapacity to conceive children.

Prior bond is by far the most common impediment to marriage. Prior bond arises when a person is already validly married and his or her spouse is still alive. Because indissolubility is one of the properties of marriage (see question 21), the Church does not recognize civil divorce. And because indissolubility falls under the natural law, the Church cannot dispense from prior bond.

The Church may, when certain circumstances are met, dissolve a natural marriage in favor of a new marriage or a sacramental marriage that has not been consummated. (Feel free to take a sneak peak at chapter eight, where we answer several questions about the circumstances under which the Church may dissolve a marriage.)

43. I was baptized Catholic as a child and still practice, but my Jewish girlfriend has never been baptized. Is this an impediment to our marrying?

Yes. Because marriage between the baptized is a sacrament, which brings about a much deeper relationship than natural marriage, the Church encourages baptized Catholics to marry baptized Christians. The impediment to marriage between a baptized Catholic and a nonbaptized individual is known as *disparity of cult*. (*Cult* in this context is an old Latin word for "worship," not the modern English term for a kooky religious sect.)

Therefore a marriage between a baptized Catholic who has not formally left the Church[1] and a nonbaptized individual is invalid. Having said that, the impediment may be dispensed by the diocesan bishop, vicar general or episcopal vicar. This requires the couple to meet three conditions. The first is that the Catholic party agrees to do his or her best to raise children born of the marriage as Catholics. The second condition is that the nonbaptized party be made aware of the Catholic party's obligation to ensure the Catholic upbringing of the children. The third condition is that the Catholic party must try to do all that can be done to remove any dangers that the Catholic might leave the Catholic faith.

The situation has arisen where a Catholic married someone commonly believed to be baptized, but the baptism was later called into doubt. In such a scenario the Church continues to assume the marriage is valid until the invalidity of the baptism is proven.

44. *I'm a fan of historical and fantasy romance novels. I read a lot of stories about knights in shining armor kidnapping fair maidens from their fathers' castles and then marrying them. While this makes for great fiction, would such a marriage be valid?*

Absolutely not. Canon 1089 establishes an impediment preventing a man from marrying a woman whom he has kid-napped for the purpose of marriage. This is known as the impediment of abduction. It applies so long as the woman is being held captive. Thus the impediment is not permanent. A woman can choose to marry her captor once she has been freed and brought to a safe place.

Star Wars fans may recall that Jabba the Hutt kidnapped Princess Leia near the beginning of *Return of the Jedi*. Had Jabba sought to marry Leia, rather than simply hold her as a slave, the marriage would be considered invalid. Canon law would permit Leia to marry Jabba validly only after Leia had been set free. (Canon 1103 states that marriages are invalid if compelled by *force*.)

Interestingly, canon 1089 is gender specific. No impedi-ment arises when a woman kidnaps a man with the purpose of marrying him. Thus, the Church would recognize a mar-riage where Princess Leia kidnapped Jabba the Hutt and brought him back to her palace on New Alderaan before Darth Vader could rescue him.

45. *You've mentioned that consanguinity is an impediment, but I know two cousins who married in the Church. How is this possible?*

Consanguinity involves various factors and degrees of rela-tionship, not all of which give rise to an impediment. In the direct line—that is, between an ancestor and his or her descen-dant (parent and child, grandparent and grandchild, great-grandparent and great-grandchild and so on)—consanguinity is always an impediment of the natural law. Thus the Church cannot dispense from it.

The collateral line is different. This concerns blood relations in which neither party is a direct descendant of the other. Thus brother and sister, niece and uncle, nephew and aunt, cousins—all involve consanguinity in the collateral line to varying degrees.

The Latin Church calculates the degree of consanguinity by numbering the parties and their ancestors all the way up to but not including the common ancestor. Thus brother and sister are in the second degree collateral (one brother, one sister, excluding common parent or parents). Aunt and nephew or uncle and niece are third-degree collateral (young man or woman, parent, sibling of parent, excluding the common ancestor). Finally, cousins are fourth-degree collateral (cousin, parent of cousin, sibling of parent, child of sibling, excluding the common grandparent or grandparents).

In the collateral line, consanguinity is an impediment up to and including the fourth degree. Thus consanguinity in the fifth degree—between a man and his cousin's daughter or a woman and her cousin's son—would not create an impediment to marriage. The Church may dispense from consanguinity in the third or fourth degree. So the cousins you mention probably obtained this dispensation before marrying.

The impediment of adoption also arises in the direct line and the second degree of the collateral line where a legal relationship exists through adoption. Thus canon law prohibits marriage between a man and his adopted daughter or a woman and her adopted grandson. Similarly, a man cannot marry a woman previously adopted by his parents. Thus the impediment applies even though no blood relationship exists.

In a similar vein (pardon the pun), the Church also recognizes the impediment of affinity. This arises through marriage and applies to the direct line. Thus a man cannot marry his mother-in-law or a woman her former husband's grandfather. However, no prohibition exists in the Latin Church to a man's marrying his sister-in-law, as this is a relationship in the collateral line.

Finally there is the impediment of public propriety. This arises when a couple have entered into an invalid marriage, lived together without the benefit of marriage or carried on a long-term sexual relationship. It applies to the direct line of the individual's former partner. Thus a woman could not marry the father or son of her ex-boyfriend if she and her ex had lived together; nor could a man, under similar circumstances, marry the mother or daughter of his ex-girlfriend.

chapter five

A Matter of Consent

46. *You mentioned marriage consent in a previous chapter. How does this consent relate to the declaration of invalidity process?*

As stated earlier, the consent of the parties brings the marriage into being. Canon lawyers use the expression "Consent makes marriage" to explain this concept. It naturally follows that a marriage cannot come into being if the consent is lacking or seriously flawed. This is where a declaration of invalidity becomes a possibility. The person initiating the process will attempt to prove before a Church tribunal that the consent of one or both parties was lacking. Canon lawyers generally refer to cases subjected to this process as "formal cases," and the process itself as "the formal process."

Consent requires three things: capacity, knowledge and willingness. Both husband and wife must be capable of giving consent at the time of their wedding; they must know what they are doing and with whom they are doing it; and they must be willing to enter into marriage as the Church teaches marriage to be. Therefore, consent also breaks down in the areas of capacity, knowledge and willingness. Every ground in a formal annulment case falls under one of these three categories, with the exception of impediments.

Keep in mind that marriage is a lifelong relationship in which the couple promise to assist and support each other in all areas of life. Such a decision should not be entered into lightly.

47. What are "psychological grounds," and how do they affect a person's ability to contract marriage validly?

A person must be capable of giving consent if he or she wishes to enter into marriage. Canon 1095 establishes grounds by which an individual lacks the capacity to give consent. The canon is broken down into three paragraphs, with each paragraph defining a different way in which an individual may lack the capacity to give consent. These three are a lack of sufficient use of reason, a grave lack of discretion of judgment (which we will discuss in the next question) and an inability to assume the essential obligations of marriage due to a psychological issue.

A lack of sufficient use of reason, as defined in the first paragraph of canon 1095, refers to a person who is not capable of making a mature decision with lifelong consequences. The cause may be permanent or temporary, natural or induced. For example, an elderly person in the advanced stages of Alzheimer's lacks sufficient use of reason due to a medical condition that is both permanent and natural.

In their ministry as canonists, Jacqui and Pete have also come across cases in which the lack of sufficient use of reason was temporary or induced. For example, a groom consumed so much alcohol or illicit drugs that he blacked out during the wedding ceremony. He has no recollection of exchanging the wedding vows. Witnesses, who were with the groom prior to the wedding ceremony, testify to the heavy drinking and drug consumption a mere hour or two before his walking down the aisle. The tribunal may find that the groom lacked the capacity to enter marriage due to a lack of sufficient use of reason.

The third paragraph of canon 1095 deals with the presence of a psychological problem that renders the party or parties unable to actually live out the partnership of life and love. An example is the chronic alcoholic who is unable to function for any length of time without a drink. He or she may be sober enough to get through the wedding but not the reception afterward. For those who have lived with someone with this disorder, it is clear that the first priority for the severe alcoholic is the addiction. He or she will squander the family budget on the addiction, even when it means the children go hungry. The relationship with the bottle comes before that with one's spouse and children or any other human relationship.

Jacqui, when discussing capacity to consent to marriage in her public talks, refers to a former cocaine addict she knows. (The individual has been drug-free for over a decade.) Jacqui once asked him whether he still stands by the decisions he made while a cocaine addict.

"Not one!" he replied. He explained that every relationship he was in and every decision he made was about the drugs—in other words, how he could use the people in his life to get the drugs that he wanted. He fully admits that had he attempted marriage at that time, he would never have had the capacity to choose marriage or live it out as a partnership of life and love.

48. I often hear the expressions "canon 1095 annulments" and "lack of due discretion." What do these expressions mean, and how do they affect marriage consent?

In the United States and Canada, the vast majority of marriage cases are investigated under paragraph 2 of canon 1095. This canon deals with a grave lack of discretion of judgment on the part of an individual concerning the essential rights and obligations of marriage. In simple terms, it is the inability of a person to critically evaluate self, the other person or the relationship when choosing marriage.

A grave lack of discretion of judgment can arise because of serious immaturity, unresolved family of origin issues, relational issues or psychological issues. The classic example used by canon lawyers to illustrate these grounds is that of two teenagers from broken and abusive homes who, six weeks into their courtship, purposely become pregnant to force a wedding. They see marriage not as a mature lifelong partnership but as an escape from a difficult home life. Neither party has maturely reflected upon marriage, its responsibilities, one's ability to undertake this relationship or the ability of the intended spouse to enter this relationship. Rather, the decision is impetuous and immature.

49. You mentioned that consent must also be based on knowledge. What if a person enters marriage out of ignorance or error?

Ignorance and error are two grounds covered in the *Code of Canon Law*.

To enter into marriage validly, a person must know what marriage is and whom he or she is marrying. As previously mentioned, marriage is permanent, exclusive, open to the procreation and education of children and ordered toward the good of the spouses. If one is ignorant or in error about any of these basic elements or properties of marriage, the validity of one's consent may be challenged before a Church tribunal. However, the degree of ignorance or error must be carefully weighed by the tribunal. Not all acts of ignorance or error lead to invalid consent.

Note the distinction between the two terms. *Ignorance* arises when a party to marriage lacks knowledge essential to valid consent. *Error,* on the other hand, arises when the individual is mistaken in his or her knowledge of something essential to marriage consent. Both terms are explained more thoroughly in subsequent questions.

50. *How does canon law define* ignorance?

According to canon 1096, ignorance invalidates matrimonial consent when one or both parties are unaware that marriage is a lifelong partnership ordered toward the procreation of children through an act of sexual cooperation. The canon further states that such ignorance cannot be presumed after the individual reaches puberty. This means that the individual must prove his or her ignorance or that of the former spouse.

While this ground seems hypothetical in today's overly sexualized culture, it still arises from time to time. The authors have encountered cases within their canonical ministry. However, professional confidentiality prevents us from sharing real examples due to their rarity.

An example from popular fiction, however, is Carrie White—the sixteen-year-old protagonist of Stephen King's breakout novel *Carrie*. She comes from an extremely fundamentalist home: The novel opens with her experiencing a menstrual cycle for the first time, which reduces her to hysterics, as she believes she is bleeding to death. It soon becomes clear that she is ignorant of the human reproductive system, despite having reached puberty. Thus ignorance would prevent Carrie from validly consenting to marriage. (Unfortunately for her classmates, it didn't invalidate her telekinetic powers, through which she burned down her school with them in it.)

51. *How does canon law define* error?

Canons 1097 to 1100 define several types of error, not all of which invalidate marital consent.

The first type is error of person. Quite simply, the individual married the wrong person. Error of person always invalidates marital consent.

An example of error of person arises with the Old Testament patriarch Jacob. He works seven years for his future father-in-law to earn the right to marry Rachel. On the wedding day Jacob realizes that his father-in-law has tricked him into marrying Rachel's older sister, Leah. Had this marriage taken place under the New Testament, the Church could easily have declared it invalid. Jacob's consent was lacking due to error of person: He believed he was marrying Rachel.

Error may also concern a quality of a person when the quality is principally intended by the other person entering the marriage. An example of such is virginity in Middle Eastern cultures. Because virginity is highly prized and assumed of all brides, a marriage might possibly be declared invalid if a groom from such a culture discovers that his bride has prior sexual experiences, and that the condition of virginity had been discussed beforehand.

Similarly, malicious deception invalidates marriage when a person deceives another in order to obtain marital consent—particularly when the deception concerns a quality that could disrupt the couple's married life (canon 1098). Going back to the previous example, malice would arise if the bride intentionally deceived her future husband into believing she was a virgin.

In short, a person must know the individual he or she intends to marry. One cannot be deceived into contracting marriage. One must know that the person one is marrying is indeed the person one intends to marry.

52. Many non-Catholics don't share the Church's theology of marriage. For example, most Protestants do not believe that marriage is a sacrament. Does the Church recognize this type of error as grounds for a declaration of invalidity?

In general the answer is no. However, canon 1099 provides exceptions to this rule under two strict conditions. The first is when the error concerns one of three essential properties of marriage–unity, indissolubility or, between two baptized people, sacramentality. The second is that the error determined the will of the party in entering the marriage.

What this means is that the person would not have attempted marriage had he or she properly understood Church teaching about unity, indissolubility or sacramentality. An example of this is the recent trend among young uncatechized couples toward so-called "starter marriages." These couples undertake marriage with the mistaken belief that they can always divorce if it does not work out. They would not marry if they understood marriage to be indissoluble. Thus, their error concerning marriage as a lifelong institution is what allows them to overcome their hesitancy to enter into this relationship.

This error invalidates the couple's marital consent because it meets the two conditions outlined in canon 1099. The error concerns an essential property of marriage, namely, indissolubility, and it determines the will of the party in contracting the marriage.

53. *Moving on to willingness, what is* simulation, *and how does it invalidate marital consent?*

A person must be willing to enter into marriage as the Church teaches it. Once again, since marriage is permanent, exclusive, open to the procreation and education of children and ordered to the good of the spouses, a person must be willing to enter into a marriage that is all of these things.

The Church presumes that the parties, in giving their consent, agree to this sort of marriage. If they intentionally exclude any or all of the above, then the parties are said to have simulated or excluded marriage (canon 1101). Simulation arises when a person says one thing while exchanging wedding vows but actually intends something else. Simulation differs from ignorance and error in that the individual understands Church teaching concerning marriage but simply chooses something else.

Simulation may be total or partial. It is total when the person completely rejects marriage. One common example in America is that of a foreigner who marries a U.S. citizen to obtain a green card. The immigrant spouse then disappears shortly after "becoming legal" in the country.

Partial simulation arises when an individual intends a marriage-type relationship with the other person but intentionally excludes an essential element or property of marriage. A common example in North America involves young couples who marry with the intention of remaining childless. This is grounds for invalidity due to the couple's partial simulation against openness to children.

The same is true of couples who agree to so-called "open marriages," in which a spouse is free to continue sexual relations with a third party. In such a case the marriage is invalid due to the couple's intention against unity (also known as intention against fidelity).

Some cultures permit "temporary" or "term" marriages, by which couples marry for an agreed time period rather than for life. These marriages also fall under partial simulation because of the individual's intention against permanence (or indissolubility).

54. What about marriages subject to a condition? Why have I heard both that they are valid and that they are invalid?

The reason you have heard differently is because the time frame of the condition affects the validity of the marriage. Because marriage is contracted in the present, it can never be subject to the fulfillment of a future condition (canon 1102). We simply don't know what the future holds until we get there. For example, a young lady from an alcoholic home marries her partner on condition that he will never consume an adult beverage. Who knows what could happen at the office Christmas party five years down the road? Thus a marriage is invalid when contracted on a condition about the future.

The answer differs when the condition concerns the past or the present. Because the past has happened and the present is happening, the condition can be objectively verified. In short, it is either fulfilled or unfulfilled. And thus the marriage is either valid or not, depending upon fulfillment of the past or present condition.

In other words, the same young lady can marry her beau on condition that he has given up all use of alcoholic beverages and is not currently drinking; this would be a valid marriage.

She can even marry him on condition that he *intends to refrain* from all use of alcoholic beverages in the future. While this last condition may seem like a future condition, it actually concerns his present intention, and thus it is valid. He *intends* (in the present) to refrain from alcohol in the future. This is not the same as he *will* refrain from alcohol in the future. The marriage is still valid should he slip sometime down the road, since at the time of the wedding he intended to refrain from alcohol, thus fulfilling the condition.

Any past or present condition placed on a marriage should receive the written consent of the local ordinary. But even without the local ordinary's permission, the condition is still acceptable, and the marriage is still valid.

55. Are "shotgun marriages" valid?

The short answer is no. According to canon 1103, a marriage is invalid when entered into because of force or fear from some external source, in which the individual sees marriage as the only means of escaping the threat.

Force is fairly self-explanatory. It concerns a threat of physical harm that is both serious and real, by someone capable of carrying it out. Fear is somewhat broader. It need not concern physical harm, although it must be serious and must be perpetuated by someone capable of carrying it out. It is also more subjective.

For example, suppose a woman finds herself pregnant outside of wedlock. Her parents tell her to marry or they will throw her out of the house and disown her. This threat rises to the level of grave fear when imposed upon a sixteen-year-old with limited education, few marketable skills and little life experience. However, the same threat is more of an inconvenience when imposed upon a woman who is thirty, financially independent and well established in her professional career, and who has lived on her own while completing university studies and working.

Fear may be reverential when a close relationship exists between the individual and someone whom the individual fears disappointing, or from whom punishment could be incurred. Using the last example, the thirty-year-old woman may have married invalidly if her relationship to her parents was more dependent, and she feared their disappointment and removing her from their estate over her premarital pregnancy.

In short, a person must be free and willing to enter into marriage. A person should not be forced into marriage or subjected externally to fearful repercussions should he or she not marry. Thus the aptly named ground of "force and fear."

56. I bought this book for a family member going through a divorce. But all this talk about impediments and grounds for invalidity has made me paranoid about the validity of my otherwise happy marriage. What should I do?

Relax. Thank God for blessing you with a wonderful spouse. Take some time to say, "Honey, I love you."

One of the most important canons pertaining to marriage is canon 1060. This canon establishes that marriage enjoys the favor of the law. For this reason, the Church assumes a marriage to be valid until its invalidity is proven. A mere doubt is not proof.

Even throughout the tribunal process, in which several doubts are presented and backed up with hard evidence, the Church continues to presume the marriage valid until the ground for invalidity is proven before two tribunals. But more on the tribunal process in chapter seven.

Moreover, in the case of marriages contracted invalidly because of an impediment or defective form, the Church presumes that the couple's consent continues until the contrary is proven. An example of defective form is a marriage presided over by an elderly priest from out of town, who happens to be related to one of the parties. In his great joy for the couple, he forgets to obtain proper delegation from the host diocese to preside over the wedding. (Question 96 explains defective form in more detail.)

Regardless, the favor of the law enjoyed by marriage governs our approach as Catholics toward this relationship.

chapter six

Who's Who in an Annulment Case?

57. Who is the petitioner?

Each marriage case begins with the parties to the marriage, namely, a petitioner and a respondent. The petitioner is the person who introduces the case to the tribunal. In other words, he or she *petitions* the tribunal to investigate his or her former marriage for alleged invalidity. The petitioner need not be Catholic or even baptized. He or she need only be a party to the marriage being investigated.

(In rare instances the promoter of justice [see question 62] can petition the tribunal to declare a marriage invalid. In fifteen years of tribunal experience, neither Jacqui nor Pete has ever come across such a case, unless we count the single example used in a canon law textbook to illustrate the possibility.)

Why might a non-Catholic seek a declaration of invalidity from the Church? Simply put, his or her previous marriage ended in divorce, and the non-Catholic now wishes to marry a Catholic. Thus the Church permits non-Catholics—and even non-Christians—to petition the tribunal concerning a previous marriage.

58. Who is the respondent in a declaration of invalidity case?

The respondent is the other party to the marriage being investigated—the divorced or separated spouse of the petitioner. He or she *responds* to the petition introduced by the petitioner.

The respondent is free to support or oppose the petition for a declaration of invalidity. In the experience of the authors, however, most respondents are indifferent or decline to get involved in the process. Nevertheless, the respondent enjoys all the rights of the petitioner. The respondent has the right to know the case against him or her, to suggest grounds, to challenge the testimony of the petitioner and witnesses and to present witnesses. The respondent can also appeal decisions with which he or she disagrees.

59. Who is the judicial vicar?

The judicial vicar is a priest or bishop appointed by the diocesan bishop to oversee the tribunal. The judicial vicar must be at least thirty years of age, and he must possess a license or doctorate in canon law. The judicial vicar is also known as the *officialis* (Canon 1420).

The judicial vicar and the diocesan bishop form one tribunal. This means the judicial vicar oversees the tribunal on behalf of the diocesan bishop and is to follow any instructions or directives handed down by the diocesan bishop. This includes instructions not to judge specific cases that the bishop wishes to judge by himself.

Canon 1420 requires every diocesan bishop to appoint a judicial vicar for his diocese, unless some other arrangement is approved by the Holy See. The judicial vicar is also a tribunal judge by virtue of his appointment. He is not to be the same individual as the vicar general, unless the diocese is small or deals only with a small number of tribunal cases.

60. What are adjutant judicial vicars?

In large dioceses the bishop may appoint adjutant judicial vicars to assist the judicial vicar in carrying out the functions of his office. These functions include appointing officials to each case, requesting the consent of another judicial vicar in cases where the petitioner and the respondent live in two different dioceses (see question 75) and any other function outlined in the *Code of Canon Law* or delegated by the diocesan bishop.

That being said, the judicial vicar and his adjutants are not automatically appointed to judge every case that comes before the tribunal. Rather they must be assigned to each case, just like any other judge among the tribunal staff.

Like the judicial vicar, adjutants must be priests or bishops, enjoy a good reputation, be at least thirty years of age and possess a license or doctorate in canon law. They are known as *vice-officiales*.

Both the judicial vicar and any adjutant judicial vicars continue to hold office when the see is vacant, that is, when the diocesan bishop has retired, transferred to another diocese or died, and his successor has not yet been named. However, the new diocesan bishop must reconfirm the appointments upon taking possession of his office.

61. What are judges and assessors?

Because the declaration of invalidity process follows a judicial procedure, individuals must be appointed in each tribunal to oversee cases, weigh the evidence presented and come to a decision. The individuals tasked with this responsibility are judges.

Judges are appointed to the tribunal by the diocesan bishop. However, it is the judicial vicar who usually appoints judges to specific cases. A judge is said to be a *sole* judge when he acts as the only judge on a case. When acting as part of a panel of three judges (or in exceptionally difficult cases, five judges), he or she is a *collegiate* judge.

Only a cleric—that is, a deacon, priest or bishop—may act as a sole judge. However, a layperson may act as a collegiate judge provided that the other judges appointed to the case are clerics. Both sole judges and collegiate judges must be of good reputation and possess a license or doctorate in canon law.

When the tribunal is collegiate, one of the judges will also be named the *ponens*. The ponens is the judge who authors the tribunal's decision in a specific case. As in civil courts, collegiate decisions are rendered according to the majority opinion of the judges. Unlike the civil courts, however, there is no obligation of the minority in a split decision to draft a dissenting opinion.

In tribunals where the number of canon lawyers is limited, the judge may also appoint two assessors in an advisory capacity. The assessors may be clerics or laypeople.

62. Who are the defender of the bond and the promoter of justice?

Civil courts have an official who prosecutes a case on behalf of the state. Depending upon the jurisdiction, this individual is known as the prosecutor, district attorney, state attorney or Crown attorney. Two officials fulfill a similar role in Church tribunals. They are the defender of the bond and the promoter of justice.

The promoter of justice represents the public good in tribunal cases. The promoter of justice is tasked with introducing cases or intervening in cases where the public good is at stake. Because marriage concerns the public good—the couple are known publicly as Mr. and Mrs. Bloggins—the promoter of justice may intervene in any case when necessary to avoid public scandal or some other danger. In fact, the promoter of justice is one of the few individuals besides the parties to the marriage who may petition a tribunal to declare the marriage invalid.

That being said, the promoter of justice seldom intervenes in declaration of invalidity cases. This is because of the presence of another official known as the defender of the bond. Every diocesan tribunal must appoint at least one defender of the bond, who represents the bond of marriage within the tribunal process. The defender of the bond is to ensure that due process is followed and that all objections to declaring the marriage invalid are brought forward. Failure to include the defender of the bond in the process automatically invalidates the decision.

The defender of the bond and the promoter of justice may intervene in a case whenever evidence is being collected from the petitioner, the respondent or their witnesses. The defender of the bond and the promoter of justice also have the right to be heard whenever a party raises an objection or question with the judges.

The defender of the bond and the promoter of justice are appointed by the diocesan bishop, either for all cases or for individual cases. The same individual may be appointed promoter of justice and defender of the bond for the diocese, but that individual cannot act in both capacities in the same case.

The defender of the bond and promoter of justice may be a cleric or a layperson. He or she must enjoy a good reputation, demonstrate both prudence and zeal in pursuing justice and possess a license or doctorate in canon law.

63. What are advocates?

An individual coming before a civil court or a criminal court has the right to representation by a lawyer—that is, a qualified expert in the law. The lawyer represents his or her client, putting forward legal arguments in the client's favor. Church courts are similar. Every petitioner and respondent has the right to be represented by an advocate—that is, a canon lawyer who argues the party's case before the tribunal. Advocates also assist the petitioner or respondent in understanding the case, in gathering evidence and in organizing the evidence to present to the tribunal. Not every case requires an advocate, but many tribunals use them to assist the parties in understanding the process and ensuring that the rights of the parties are protected.

Canon 1483 lays out the following requirements for advocates: They must be at least eighteen years of age, be of good reputation, be a Catholic or have the permission of the diocesan bishop, possess a doctorate in canon law or show expertise in the field (the vast majority of dioceses accept a license in canon law) and receive approval from the diocesan bishop. A party may have more than one advocate in a case.

The advocate for the petitioner will, of course, argue for the marriage's invalidity. After all, the petitioner is the party asking the tribunal to declare the marriage invalid. One of the first duties of this advocate is to help petition the tribunal for an investigation of the marriage.

In contrast, the role of advocate for the respondent depends upon the respondent's wishes in most cases. The advocate for the respondent will argue in favor of the declaration of invalidity if the respondent supports the petition, and against the petition if the respondent opposes a declaration of invalidity (or the grounds cited in the petition), or the advocate will simply ensure that the respondent is being fairly represented in the process and that his or her rights are respected. This latter scenario arises when the respondent does not oppose a declaration of invalidity in principle but objects to some of the evidence presented by the petitioner or witnesses favorable to the petitioner.

From Pete and Jacqui's experience, it is not unusual for the respondent to change positions midway through a case—usually from opposing a declaration of invalidity to supporting it. When this happens the advocate for the respondent will present the respondent's new position before the tribunal.

In some countries the party must seek out and hire an advocate, as one hires a lawyer in a civil case. The advocate is then required to present a mandate to the local tribunal, as well as seek the approval of the diocesan bishop to act in the case. However, because not every individual can afford an advocate, every diocese keeps a list of advocates who receive compensation from the tribunal, similar to public defenders in North American civil courts. The tribunal may also appoint an advocate to act on behalf of the respondent in order to ensure respect for the respondent's rights when he or she cannot be located or refuses to participate in the process.

Most cases in North America don't require the participation of an advocate. However, where an advocate is deemed necessary, or where a party requests the services of an advocate, the general practice is to provide the party with the list of advocates approved by the diocese. The party is also free to hire an advocate from outside the diocese.

64. What are auditors?

Auditors are appointed by the tribunal to collect evidence on behalf of the judge. The word *auditor* comes from the Latin verb *audire*, which means "to hear." Thus an auditor hears the evidence presented by the parties and their witnesses, asking questions and recording the answers for the judges. Canon 1561 requires that the auditor be assisted by a notary when auditing (hearing evidence) and that any questions from other court officials or the parties be asked through the auditor.

To become an auditor one must first receive approval from the diocesan bishop (canon 1428). Auditors may be chosen from among clergy or laity. They must be prudent, of sound character and faithful to Church teaching.

65. What are notaries?

A notary on a Church tribunal fulfills a role similar to that of a court reporter and public notary within the civil courts. Basically a notary is responsible for notarizing public documents. That is, the notary attests through his or her signature that documents prepared for a case are accurate and that the signatures of parties or tribunal officials are authentic.

Canon 1437 requires the notary to take part in the tribunal process. This requirement is so strong that the canon declares invalid any judicial act or document that does not bear the notary's signature. Thus notaries are important to the integrity of the tribunal process. Most tribunals have several notaries who may be called upon to notarize documents and signatures at any stage of the process.

66. What are procurators?

A procurator is an individual who obtains tribunal documents on behalf of the petitioner or the respondent. The procurator must acquire a mandate from the party to act in this capacity, which the procurator then presents to the tribunal.

The requirements for procurator are similar to those for advocate: A procurator must be at least eighteen years of age and enjoy a good reputation (canon 1483). However, the procurator need not be a Catholic or an expert in canon law, nor does the procurator require approval from the diocesan bishop.

The role of procurator (sometimes called a "proxy") is often –though not always–paired with the role of advocate. Thus it is not unusual for a petitioner or respondent to appoint the same canon lawyer as both procurator and advocate. There are two advantages to having an individual act in both capacities. The first is that the petitioner or the respondent has to deal with only one person throughout the process. The second is that the procurator-advocate can act immediately upon receiving correspondence from the tribunal.

The procurator can obtain a special mandate from the party to act on his or her behalf in taking specific actions within the case. These actions include renouncing a case that appears hopeless, petitioning for a change of grounds if new evidence comes to light and appealing decisions with which the party or advocate disagrees (canon 1485).

67. What are guardians or curators?

Sometimes a person lacks sufficient maturity or mental competence to undertake the processes and decisions involved in a trial. In cases such as this, canon law requires that the tribunal appoint a guardian or curator to make decisions on behalf of the party incapable of acting on his or her own behalf.

Canon 1478 identifies two types of people for whom a guardian or curator should be appointed within the process. The first are minors, most of whom have yet to gain the knowledge and experience necessary to understand decisions that will affect them for the rest of their lives. The second are those who habitually—that is, in their normal day-to-day affairs—lack the use of reason due to advanced age, mental health issues and so on. The second situation is more common in the tribunal process.

For example, a marriage ended several decades ago, both parties have since entered new relationships and remarried civilly, and now the petitioner wishes to return to the sacraments before dying. Unfortunately, the respondent is in the advanced stages of Alzheimer's. So the tribunal can appoint a guardian to act in the respondent's place.

Guardians and curators need not be appointed from a Church list. Canon 1479 allows the tribunal judge to recognize a guardian or curator appointed by the civil authority. If possible the judge should consult with the party's bishop before recognizing a civilly appointed curator or guardian. However, there is no point in reinventing the wheel when a civil authority has appointed an elderly person's family member to manage his or her civil affairs. If the family member is competent and fair, then the Church can extend his or her guardianship to the elderly individual's ecclesiastical affairs.

68. *What are court experts?*

Court experts are clergy or laity with expertise that can help judges and other tribunal officials better understand serious issues that arise in a broken relationship. Unlike assessors, who help a judge assess an overall case, the expertise of court experts is specific to a particular issue within a case.

For example, a tribunal will often call upon psychologists, psychiatrists and other psychological experts when alcoholism, mental illness, abuse or other serious psychological issues contribute to the breakdown of a marriage. The expert will review the proceedings, interview the parties if necessary and help tribunal officials understand how various psychological factors harmed the relationship.

Other experts might be called in for other types of cases. For example, a case may involve a party serving in the military, which has its own particular subculture. When the military jargon and circumstances become a little thick—and thus difficult to understand for a tribunal official with little military experience—then the tribunal may call upon the expertise of a retired officer or senior noncommissioned member to explain the military subculture in civilian terms. The same is true of any other subculture or profession.

Thus experts help court officials better understand a case by clarifying various issues that may affect the case's outcome. Nevertheless, one must remember that court experts fulfill an advisory role. The final decision in any case rests with the judge or judges.

chapter seven

Formal Process for a Declaration of Invalidity

69. I've been married before, and I want to marry again in the Catholic Church. How do I start the declaration of invalidity process?

The first thing you need to do is contact your pastor. Let him know you are interested in possibly pursuing this process, and find out what help is available through the diocese or parish (see question 9).

The next thing on the agenda is to begin collecting documentation of your marriage. Obtain copies of your and your former spouse's baptismal certificates, marriage license/application/certificate, divorce/dissolution decree or civil annulment. If you cannot find the baptismal record for your former spouse, the tribunal will attempt to find a copy. What's more important is that you have the basic documents concerning your baptism (if you have been baptized) and all relevant civil documents. Other important documents include copies of restraining orders, arrest records and public documents that might support claims made in the testimony presented to the tribunal.

It doesn't matter if the marriage lasted 120 hours or 120 years: This information for all marriages must be presented to the tribunal for evaluation. (Yes, the Church must investigate each of your previous marriages). A civil annulment is not equivalent to the Catholic Church's declaration of invalidity, so any marriage that has been civilly annulled (or declared null by a religious body other than the Catholic Church) still needs to be evaluated. This means you will have to present the documents mentioned, insofar as they are obtainable.

Once all of the documentation is collected, or as much of it as can be found, then make a list of the names, addresses and contact information of anyone you believe can provide important information about your previous marriage.

70. Can I name my parents as witnesses? What about siblings and close friends?

Absolutely! Your list should include family members, long-time friends and others who can act as witnesses to the marriage. The best witnesses are those closest to you or your former spouse, those who have known you the best and the longest. Immediate family members are obviously the best witnesses, as they would be aware of your home life and any issues from your family of origin and upbringing.

After family members, look at who your friends were at that time—who you worked with, socialized with and confided in, who were in your wedding party. Remember, the tribunal is looking primarily at the time prior to your wedding, especially the courtship and engagement. So name witnesses who knew you well and were highly involved in your life as a dating and engaged couple.

71. What do I do with all of this information once I've collected it?

Once you have gathered the documents and listed the names and addresses of your witnesses, it's time to make another appointment with your parish priest. Please be sure, when making the appointment, to mention what it is about. This is helpful for two reasons:

1. Your priest will want to block out enough time from his schedule to assist you pastorally. This is rarely possible during a five-minute meeting after Sunday Mass, when the priest is focused on other things.
2. Your priest—or whoever at your parish is in charge of assisting with declaration of invalidity cases—will want to prepare before the appointment. So giving the parish secretary a "heads up" helps ensure that the meeting runs more smoothly and pastorally.

At the appointment your parish priest or his representative will work with you to complete the proper paperwork. He will help you prepare a petition to the tribunal, which begins the formal declaration of invalidity process. This happens once the paperwork is forwarded to the tribunal along with any requested processing fees.

In some dioceses, the parties approach the tribunal directly rather than go through their parish. The tribunal will have specific personnel who can meet with people who are considering filing for a declaration of invalidity and who will help them with the appropriate paperwork. It is best, however, to start by approaching your parish priest, in order to start the process in the most pastoral way possible. However, every person is permitted to approach the tribunal directly.

72. What happens once everything is forwarded to the tribunal?
Different dioceses handle cases in different ways, although there is one *Code of Canon Law* and one official process. In

most North American dioceses, once the tribunal has received your initial paperwork, you will be asked to begin working on your personal history. This can be done in several ways, but the usual method is either a written questionnaire or an interview with the tribunal staff.

Some dioceses ask very open-ended questions, looking for long narratives. Other dioceses send out questionnaires with very specific questions requiring shorter yet still detailed answers. It is important to be as detailed as possible about your life. As mentioned previously, the tribunal is not so much concerned about how the marriage ended as whether there were any problems prior to the wedding that were unresolved before the marriage.

So share as much detail as you can about your family of origin and your relationship with your parents and siblings prior to the wedding, as well as their relationships with each other. Talk about family dynamics and anything that might have been out of the ordinary, like patterns of divorce and remarriage, abuse or addictive behaviors.

Talk about your dating history, both with your former spouse and others whom you dated prior to the wedding. How did your former spouse get along with your friends and family? Did anyone warn you or express concerns prior to your wedding day? Was there a pregnancy involved, and did that affect your decision to marry? The tribunal will want to know about any such issues from your past.

The tribunal will also ask you questions about your courtship, the engagement period and the early part of your common life as husband and wife. Was the adjustment to marriage easy? Did you go on a honeymoon, and if so, were there any unusual incidents? While knowing what happened later in the marriage is both important and beneficial to the tribunal, knowing what happened during the courtship, engagement and early part of the marriage is critical.

Of course, you likely won't be able to finish your personal history in one sitting, unless your diocese uses an oral interview format with a tribunal staff member. The tribunal understands that revisiting the past taxes one emotionally, thus requiring a tremendous amount of energy. Take as many sittings as you need to complete your personal history.

73. What about my former spouse's personal history? Should I include information about that as well?

Absolutely. Marriage is a covenant between two people. Therefore both individuals have to approach marriage with sufficient maturity and the right attitude. Consequently the tribunal will want to know about your former spouse. What was his or her childhood like? What type of relationship did he or she enjoy with parents, siblings and other family members? Any divorce, addictions or abuse in your former spouse's family? How did in-laws impact your relationship after the wedding?

Be fair to your former spouse, but provide the tribunal with as much information as you can about his or her family background.

74. What happens after I turn in my personal history?

At this time your petition will be reviewed and submitted to the tribunal. The petition is a statement in which you specify the reason you are asking the tribunal to investigate your marriage for alleged invalidity. The petition will state the grounds

—that is, the alleged cause of the invalidity—as well as the individual on whose part the grounds apply. For example, if you list as your grounds "partial simulation due to the respondent's intention against children," then you are asking the tribunal to declare your marriage invalid because your former spouse did not want to have children when you wed.

Don't fret if the prospect of drafting a petition seems overwhelming. Someone from the tribunal staff, and possibly your advocate, will help you determine what grounds are best suited to your case. Additionally, depending on the evidence gathered and presented throughout the process, these grounds can be amended should more suitable grounds become known within the process.

Once the tribunal receives the case, the judicial vicar will decide whether the tribunal has competency over the case (see next question). If yes, the judicial vicar will appoint a judge or panel of judges, a defender of the bond, any other required officials and notaries. At this point the tribunal is not making a judgment on the merits of the case—that is, determining whether sufficient evidence exists to rule the marriage invalid. The tribunal is simply stating it has competency to hear the case, and thus the case can move forward to trial.

The judge will then contact your former spouse and ask him or her to respond to the petition. See questions 76 to 78 for more information on contacting the respondent.

75. You mentioned that the tribunal must first determine competency over a case. What does this mean, and why is this important?
Imagine if a person could introduce a legal case before any court. This would lead to chaos as complainants shopped around for courts favorable to their cause, even courts that

had no connection to the individuals involved in the case. For instance, a large business in New York could sue one of its customers in a California court, knowing the customer lacked the financial resources to travel regularly to California and defend himself.

To avoid similar types of situations in the Church, a tribunal must first establish its legal competency to hear a case. That is, a tribunal must have some sort of connection to the case to justify hearing it. If a tribunal proceeds despite being absolutely incompetent to hear a case, then any actions that follow from the case are invalid.

Canon 1673 establishes competency to hear a case in the following order:

1. The tribunal of the diocese where the wedding took place.

2. The tribunal of the place where the respondent has a permanent residence or a temporary residence of at least three months.

3. The tribunal of the place where the petitioner lives, provided certain circumstances are met. The first is that the petitioner and respondent must live under the same conference of bishops. For example, this is possible if one party is living in Hawaii and the other in Maine, because both states fall under the United States Conference of Catholic Bishops. However, the same is not true if one former spouse is living in Puerto Rico and the other in southeastern Florida. Despite the closer proximity than in the previous example, Puerto Rico has its own episcopal conference.

The second condition is that the judicial vicar of the diocese where the respondent resides must give his consent after consulting with the respondent.

4. The tribunal where most of the evidence can be gathered. This, too, requires the consent of the respondent's judicial vicar after consulting with the respondent.

For example, suppose a newlywed Chinese couple escape to the United States with extended families in tow. Everyone settles in the archdiocese of Atlanta, Georgia, where they become naturalized U.S. citizens. A few years later the couple move to North Dakota, where the marriage falls apart. The couple could choose to have the case heard by the archdiocese of Atlanta tribunal, since this is where they originally immigrated to, where they became U.S. citizens and where the majority of the witnesses (friends and family) still live.

Finally, because such cases are politically and pastorally sensitive, and to avoid undue influence on the process by the state, only the pope can judge a case involving the highest official in a state (canon 1405 §1). In the United States this means the U.S. president. In Canada this applies to the governor general. (For non-Canadian readers, Canada separates its head of state and its head of government. The governor general fulfills the role of head of state in the absence of the queen, while the prime minister is head of government.)

76. Does my former spouse have to be contacted?
Yes, it is a requirement of canon law that your former spouse be contacted. The marriage was your former spouse's as well,

so he or she has every right to participate fully in the process. The respondent has the right to know the grounds for seeking a declaration of invalidity and to respond to those grounds: to share his or her side of the story, usually through answering questions posed by the tribunal, to respond to the evidence presented and to present witnesses to the tribunal.

Now, this does not mean that the tribunal is going to give any information about you to the respondent. You have your right to privacy, and most tribunals will refer to you by your maiden name if you are a woman. The tribunal also will not release your current contact information to the respondent, such as your address or telephone number, if the person specifically requests this and has a good reason for the request.

In our experience most respondents choose not to participate. Of those that do, some will support the petition, some will oppose it, and others just want to share their side of the story and leave the decision up to the tribunal. Pete has even participated in cases in which the petitioner and respondent, having remained friends after the divorce, insisted that they be interviewed together. Pete had to explain to them that by law they were to be heard separately. However, any interviews with the tribunal will come later in the process.

77. What if my former spouse has a history of violent abuse, making me fear for the physical safety of my children and me?

If you fear for your physical safety, please be sure to inform the tribunal of this fact. The tribunal will likely want you to back up this fear with some sort of evidence that the respondent is volatile or has a propensity for violence. So make copies of documents like emergency protection orders, restraining orders, police reports, photographs taken after a previous violent outburst or convictions for crimes of violence imposed by a secular court. Copies of the aforementioned documents may also provide additional insight or evidence into the breakdown of your marriage, depending upon how far back the violence goes and what grounds are being alleged in the petition.

The tribunal will do all that is within its power to protect the privacy of you and your children from anyone, including a respondent who is known to be violent. The key point to remember is this: On the one hand, the Church does not wish to put any individual into a situation where he or she risks becoming the victim of further violence; this is true regardless of whether the individual at risk is the petitioner, the respondent (sometimes the petitioner is the violent party) or their children. On the other hand, natural justice requires that the respondent be given a reasonable opportunity to answer the allegations. The Church will do its best to balance both needs in these types of situations.

78. If my former spouse refuses to participate, does this mean that my process must stop?

No, the process will not stop, or be abated, merely because the respondent refuses to participate. In fact, as previously mentioned, most respondents choose not to participate. If such is the case with your former spouse, the tribunal may continue with the case after giving the respondent suitable time to respond. The time frame depends upon how far along the case is.

Upon receiving a copy of the petition, the petitioner and the respondent have fifteen days to respond if he or she feels the grounds should be changed or added to. The time frame can be longer if the respondent is out of town, in the hospital or facing some personal crisis or emergency.

Some respondents will state early in the process that they wish to participate, then do nothing but slow down the process by being obstinate or problematic in other ways, such as demanding extension after extension for filing paperwork or *repeatedly* canceling appointments at the last moment. Sometimes the petitioner is the one who drags out the process, forcing a respondent who supports the petition to take charge of the case. Regardless, the parties have the right to have their marriage evaluated by the tribunal. The testimony and evidence will still be gathered.

If the respondent has failed to participate after deadlines have passed, then the case will proceed without his or her input. Moreover, the judge may declare the respondent judicially absent from the proceedings. The same is true of the petitioner in cases where he or she has lost interest but the respondent continues to pursue the case. Of course, the case stalls if neither party is interested in moving it forward.

79. What is the joinder of issues?

After the respondent replies to the grounds—assuming he or she takes the opportunity to do so—comes the *joinder of issues*. At this stage of the process, the presiding judge joins the petitioner's petition and the respondent's response and issues a decree outlining the grounds upon which the tribunal will investigate the marriage.

For example, suppose a man petitions the tribunal to declare his marriage invalid because his former wife refused to bring children into the relationship. Thus he alleges that his former wife partially simulated her consent because she harbored an intention against children at the time of the couple's wedding. Upon receiving a copy of the petition, the woman replies that her husband was a severe alcoholic. The respondent hoped that her former husband would grow out of it once the couple married, but it never happened. Thus she refused to bring children into a relationship where the petitioner could not hold down a job, became emotionally and physically abusive whenever he drank and squandered the family budget on his alcohol addiction.

Having heard from both sides, the judge may join the issues by decreeing that the tribunal will investigate the marriage on the following grounds: incapacity to assume the essential obligations of marriage, due to causes of a psychological nature (alcohol addiction) on the part of the former husband (canon 1095, paragraph 3), and partial simulation, due to an intention against children on the part of the respondent (canon 1101, paragraph 2). Thus the joinder of issues decree brings together the reasons for investigating the case.

80. What happens after the judge presents the joinder of issues?
Once the grounds have been determined by the judge, a call to trial follows. This is the stage at which the tribunal collects evidence. The judges will review your personal history. If need be, they will ask you to clarify certain details or provide additional information. Any judge may do this personally or through an auditor.

Additionally, if the respondent wishes to participate in the process, the tribunal will contact him or her for any clarifications or additional information needed. The witnesses will be contacted as well and asked to give their testimony. The questions they are asked will likely not be as detailed as the ones the petitioner and the respondent had to answer.

If you name any doctors or therapists as witnesses, the tribunal will ask you to sign a consent form. This allows the doctors or therapists to release to the tribunal pertinent information from your medical or counseling background. This information often proves helpful to a case—particularly those involving the psychological grounds outlined in canon 1095 (see question 47). Other evidence is also gathered at this time.

81. What happens after the evidence is gathered?

Once the evidence is gathered, the tribunal publishes the acts of the case. Don't worry; your life story won't appear on Amazon.com for complete strangers to purchase. "Publication" in this context simply means that the tribunal makes the evidence available to the petitioner and respondent for comment. The evidence collected along with all the other legal actions of the tribunal are known as "the acts of the case" (or simply "the acts").

The judges may ask the parties follow-up questions at this time, after which the case is closed, and no more new testimony is accepted by the tribunal. The tribunal then passes the acts to the advocates for the petitioner and the respondent. The advocates, if there are any, must review the acts and submit a brief to the tribunal supporting the positions held by the parties they represent.

As previously mentioned, the petitioner and respondent could both favor a declaration of invalidity. Therefore it is quite possible that both advocates might file similar briefs arguing for the same outcome, namely, that the marriage be declared invalid on the grounds being investigated. Or if the parties differ, the advocates will find themselves writing opposing briefs.

Once the advocates have submitted their briefs, a copy of the acts—including the advocates' briefs—is given to the defender of the bond for review. It is the defender of the bond's job to do exactly what the name implies—defend the bond of marriage. So unlike a divorce case, in which two parties act in opposition to each other, a tribunal case involves three parties: the petitioner, the respondent and the defender of the bond. The petitioner alleges the invalidity of the marriage, while the defender of the bond defends the validity of the marriage. The respondent puts forward his or her position, and may agree with the petitioner or the defender of the bond, or may offer some third position.

The defender of the bond likewise examines the acts and submits a brief to the tribunal. The defender's brief will assert the validity of the marriage, point out where canon law may not have been rigorously observed during the processing of the case and question the accuracy or applicability of the evidence presented. Perhaps the defender of the bond feels that too much weight was given to a witness who hardly knew the couple before their wedding day. Or perhaps the defender of the bond feels a respondent declared absent from the proceedings was not given an adequate overview of the process prior to declining.

82. When do the judges finally see the case?

The defender of the bond adds his brief to the acts and submits the entire package to the judge or judges. If the case is being directed by a single judge, then he will review the acts and write his decision. (Remember that only a cleric—that is, a deacon, priest or bishop—can serve as a single judge.) If the tribunal is collegiate, then the three judges (or more in exceptionally difficult cases) will each review the acts and will write up their own decisions. The judge chosen as the *ponens* will then write the final judgment on behalf of the tribunal.

The decision may be affirmative, that is to say, that the marriage has been proven invalid. The judge (or majority of judges in the case of a collegiate tribunal) must be *morally certain* of the marriage's invalidity. Moral certitude means that there exists no reasonable doubt suggesting otherwise.

The decision may also be negative. This means that the marriage has not been proven invalid to the moral certitude of the sole judge or of a majority of collegiate judges. In fact, canon law requires the judge to uphold the presumption of a valid marriage, as per canon 1060, if he remains uncertain after reviewing the acts as to whether the alleged invalidity of the marriage has been proven.

The decision is then published: That is, the parties and their advocates are notified of the court's ruling.

83. Once the tribunal decides that my marriage is invalid, am I free to marry?

Actually, you are not free to marry after one affirmative decision. To ensure that justice has truly been served, the *Code of Canon Law* requires two affirmative decisions. Therefore, any affirmative decision is automatically sent on appeal to a tribunal of second instance (an appeal court), which can confirm the decision of the first tribunal or admit the case to a full hearing. The latter means that the second instance tribunal hears the whole case again. The result of a full hearing can either be an affirmative decision or a negative one.

In the United States all dioceses are part of an ecclesiastical province overseen by an archdiocese. The second-instance tribunal is generally the tribunal of the archdiocese that oversees the ecclesiastical province to which the diocese of first instance belongs. When a case comes before the archdiocesan tribunal at first instance, then the second-instance tribunal is generally the tribunal of the oldest suffragan diocese, that is, the oldest diocese within the ecclesiastical province.

That being said, other accommodations may be made with Rome's approval. For instance, Canada has a single second-instance tribunal for the entire country. This tribunal is located in Ottawa, which is the nation's capital.

Only when you receive a second affirmative decision from a higher tribunal are you free to attempt a new marriage. If the second-instance tribunal comes back with a negative decision, you may appeal to the Roman Rota—one of the Church's two supreme courts—for a third evaluation. You also can appeal to the court of second instance or the Roman Rota if you receive a negative decision from the first-instance tribunal.

84. What if I'm the respondent and I disagree with the affirmative decision? What are my options?

If the first-instance decision comes back affirmative, and you disagree as the respondent, you may appeal to the second-instance tribunal for a full hearing or appeal directly to the Roman Rota. Likewise, the defender of the bond may also appeal to the second-instance tribunal for a full hearing or appeal directly to the Roman Rota. You need not be a Catholic to appeal; you simply need to be a party to the case.

The cost of an appeal to Rome is approximately $850 as of the time of the writing of this book, which is often cost-prohibitive to many.

Additionally, the respondent remains the respondent at higher instances, even when he or she is the source of an appeal. This is in contrast to many secular jurisdictions, where the defendant becomes the complainant if the defendant appeals to a higher court. Thus, the respondent retains his or her rights throughout the entire process. Because marriage enjoys the favor of the law and because defending one's marriage is a right within the Church, a respondent cannot be forced to bear the entire cost of the appeal.

If you are a respondent and wish to appeal an affirmative decision, simply inform the tribunal that issued the decision of your intention to appeal to either the second-instance tribunal or the Roman Rota.

85. If the tribunal decision comes back negative and appeal isn't possible, can I introduce another case?

Yes, a second case can be introduced. However, there is one condition: The new case cannot allege the same ground on the part of the same party.

For instance, suppose you're a woman whose parents forced you to marry as a teenager after you came home pregnant. Your marriage was off to a rocky start, never stabilized, and nobody is surprised years later when the relationship breaks down completely. After the divorce is finalized, you petition the tribunal to declare your marriage invalid, alleging force and fear (canon 1103) on your part because of the "shotgun" nature of the wedding. Unfortunately, most of your immediate family members have passed away, and few other witnesses are available. Therefore the decision comes back negative due to lack of evidence.

You cannot introduce a second case alleging force and fear on your part. You may introduce a case alleging force and fear on the part of the respondent, if your former husband was also forced into the marriage (assuming, of course, that this ground was not alleged against him too during the first case). You may allege another ground against yourself, such as grave lack of discretion of judgment (canon 1095, paragraph 2), stating you felt undue *internal* pressure to marry (force and fear concerns undue *external* pressure to marry). So, provided you change the reason for alleging invalidity, or the person against whom the allegation is focused, you can introduce a second case before the tribunal if the decision in your first case comes back negative.

Interestingly enough, this question often comes not from former petitioners but from former respondents. It is not unusual for a petitioner to approach the tribunal shortly after the couple's divorce is finalized, while many of the wounds are still open. The respondent will oppose a declaration of invalidity during the first case, successfully appeal at second or third instance for a negative decision and then go his or her own way. A few years later the respondent will meet a new love interest and seek to reopen the case. Because reopening a case requires a difficult and lengthy process, most tribunals prefer to start a new case.

86. I received two affirmative decisions without any further appeals, yet the tribunal tells me I am still not free to attempt another marriage. What are a monitum and a vetitum?

Just because a person's previous marriage was declared invalid doesn't mean that the person is ready to attempt another marriage. Quite often the unresolved issues that were brought into the first relationship, and that contributed to that relationship's breakdown, remain after the divorce. The Church wants to make sure you deal with these issues appropriately before allowing you to attempt another marital relationship.

Toward this end a tribunal may impose a *monitum* or *vetitum* upon one or both parties. A *monitum* is the lesser of the two impositions. In general, a *monitum* is a warning to the pastor or the person charged with preparing the new couple for marriage. The *monitum* might state that the petitioner's previous marriage was declared invalid due to her belief that marriage can end by divorce if the couple isn't happy. Therefore the priest is asked to spend extra time with the petitioner explaining the Church's teaching that marriage is permanent and indissoluble.

Or suppose a respondent is a recovering alcoholic who sobered up after the divorce several years before. A *monitum* might ask the pastor to ensure that the respondent has not had any lapses with the bottle prior to attempting another marriage.

A *vetitum* is much more serious. It is not only a warning but a prohibition against another attempt at marriage. In general a *vetitum* requires that the party perform some action before the tribunal will remove it. For instance, the tribunal might require an alcoholic to show a year of unbroken sobriety. An abusive spouse may be required to undergo anger management as well as submit to a relationship evaluation with his or her intended spouse before a licensed therapist.

In short, the *monitum* and *vetitum* protect the integrity of marriage, helping to ensure that the petitioner or respondent doesn't repeat the same mistakes in a subsequent marriage.

chapter eight

Other Options

87. Is a declaration of invalidity the only option for resolving a prior marriage, or are other options available?

Under certain circumstances options other than the formal process become available. These options are as follows: lack of canonical form, ligamen (prior bond), Pauline Privilege, or Favor of the Faith and canonical separation. We will explain each of these possibilities in more detail in subsequent questions, listing the circumstances under which they become available.

Having said that, there is another option that—sadly—is often overlooked by couples and those in ministry. It is the option of repairing one's marriage. Canon 1676 is clear: Prior to accepting a petition, the judge should, whenever possible, use pastoral means to urge the couple toward reconciliation and the healing of their marriage.

Many marriages break down not because of serious mental or physical abuse, to which nobody should be subjected, but because of little things that cause the couple to grow dissatisfied with each other. Perhaps the couple have lost touch emotionally and forgotten how to communicate their love to one another. Perhaps the couple feel like roommates sharing parental duties, the flames of romance having died after the birth of their last child through the tedium of day-to-day responsibilities. We cannot count the times we have read the following testimony from a petitioner or respondent: "My former spouse was a good person and an excellent parent to our children. We simply grew apart/fell out of love/couldn't communicate with each other." These marriages can often be repaired if the couples are motivated to fix them. But a couple must do so together.

Patrick and Nancy Madrid and Greg and Julie Alexander are two examples of couples who healed their marriages after seriously contemplating divorce. Patrick shares his and Nancy's story in the book *Surprised by Truth 2*, explaining how the couple's decision to turn back to God saved their marriage and eventually led Patrick to become a lay Catholic evangelist. The same is true of Greg and Julie Alexander, whose marriage had fallen apart and who were inquiring into the declaration of invalidity process when the judicial vicar for their diocese helped them rediscover their Catholic faith. Greg and Julie share their story in *Surprised by Truth 3*.[1] Today the couple operate Alexander House (TheAlexander House.org), a Texas-based apostolate that helps couples live according to Catholic teaching.

Of course, marriages with more serious problems can also be healed. However, they will require a lot of work on the part of spouses. For example, an alcoholic may have to undergo treatment for addiction and show a period of stability. A person prone to domestic violence will have to take anger management classes and learn nonviolent ways of communicating. Or if financial irresponsibility is driving the couple apart, the marriage might be saved through credit counseling and learning how to draft a family budget and stick to it. Each of these cases will require the constant effort of both parties to the marriage.

88. My spouse and I are separated [or divorced]. There was no abuse or mistreatment in our marriage: We simply grew apart due to different work schedules, our children's needs and other demands on our time. We stopped paying attention to each other and found we could no longer communicate. Is it too late to save our marriage?

Not if both of you feel your marriage is worth saving and are willing to put in the effort to save it. Anyone serious about saving a marriage—whether the spouses are currently living under the same roof in a loveless union, are separated or are divorced—should check out a good program called Retrouvaille (Retrouvaille.org).

Retrouvaille is the French word for "rediscovery." It describes itself as a program offering couples "the tools needed to rediscover a loving marriage relationship. Thousands of couples headed for cold, unloving relationships or divorce have successfully overcome their marriage problems by attending the program."

"The main emphasis of the program is on communication in marriage between husband and wife," says Deacon Eugene Perabo, a facilitator with Retrouvaille in Ottawa, Canada. Many of the couples who approach the program have found themselves unable to communicate with each other, Eugene told the authors.

Program facilitators usually include a Catholic priest or deacon along with two or three couples who have been through the program before. These couples share their experiences, describing the difficult times they faced within their own marriages and how they overcame these obstacles. They coach attending couples who are willing to invest the time and energy to work through similar difficulties.

Retrouvaille is just one of many programs available through the Church for couples experiencing marital difficulties. Your parish priest or diocesan family life office may know of others.

89. Can a marriage be dissolved? How does dissolution differ from a declaration of invalidity?

Only God can dissolve a marriage that is both sacramental and has been consummated after becoming a sacrament. People marry "until death do us part," meaning that God eventually dissolves a marriage through the death of one of the spouses. This has not gone unnoticed by unscrupulous individuals who brought about the death of their spouse so that they could remarry. Which is why the Church, in her wisdom, established the impediment of crime (see question 39).

Having said that, the Church has means of dissolving marriages that are not sacramental *or* have not been consummated. These means are known as the Pauline Privilege, Favor of the Faith and non-consummation cases. In each of these the old marriage is dissolved in favor of a new marriage.

A dissolution differs from a declaration of invalidity in one important respect. With a declaration of invalidity, the Church says that the relationship entered into by the couple never became a marriage despite the external appearances of marriage. In contrast, the Church recognizes the validity of a marriage that it dissolves.

90. What is the Pauline Privilege?

The Pauline Privilege is the process by which the Church dissolves a natural marriage entered into by two persons proven to not be baptized, one of whom subsequently receives baptism. The dissolution must take place in favor of a new marriage. The privilege is named after Saint Paul, who instructed early Christians:

> To the rest I say, not the Lord, that if any brother has a wife who is an unbeliever, and she consents to live with him, he should not divorce her. If any woman has a husband who is an unbeliever, and he consents to live with her, she should not divorce him. For the unbelieving husband is consecrated through his wife, and the unbelieving wife is consecrated through her husband. Otherwise, your children would be unclean, but as it is they are holy. But if the unbelieving partner desires to separate, let it be so; in such a case the brother or sister is not bound. For God has called us to peace. (1 Corinthians 7:12–15)

Four conditions must be met before the Pauline Privilege can apply:

1. Both parties must not have been baptized at the time of their wedding.
2. One of the parties must receive baptism into the Christian faith at some point after the wedding, even after the divorce, and that this baptized party cannot have been the cause of the marital breakdown after becoming baptized.
3. The nonbaptized spouse must refuse to "live in peace" with the spouse who has received baptism. Refusal to live in peace includes the refusal to live with the Christian spouse or to respect the Christians spouse's right to practice the Christian faith.
4. The Christian spouse must seek a dissolution of the old marriage in favor of a new marriage.

Evidence of the above is collected by the local ordinary or whomever he delegates to process the privilege on his behalf. In many dioceses the local ordinary will delegate the tribunal. If possible, the Church will contact the non-Christian spouse to determine whether he or she is willing to live in peace with the Christian party (canon 1144). This questioning of the non-Christian spouse should take place after the baptism of the Christian spouse; however, the bishop can permit this questioning to be done before the baptism or not at all if there is evidence that it cannot be done or otherwise would be useless.

Once all the evidence is collected and the above four conditions are met, the local ordinary can permit the new marriage to take place. Of course, the non-Christian spouse is similarly free to contract a new marriage once the first marriage has been dissolved.

91. *What if the baptized spouse wishes to contract a new marriage with a non-Christian? What if the Christian party converts from a polygamous culture? Or what if the Christian spouse is fleeing persecution in his or her homeland and cannot restore cohabitation with the non-Christian spouse? Is the Pauline Privilege still possible under these circumstances?*

Yes to all these instances.

Beginning with the first scenario, the local ordinary may allow the party who receives Christian baptism to contract a marriage with a non-Christian should a grave reason present itself (canon 1147). Canon law does not define "grave reason" but leaves it to the judgment of the local ordinary. Perhaps a person divorced, then married another non-Christian in a civil ceremony prior to receiving baptism, and the two remain happily married. Perhaps this second marriage has produced children who are living at home. Breaking up the couple would pose great harm to the children. Thus the local ordinary can permit the application of the Pauline Privilege with a second nonbaptized spouse. Of course, this is not a practice the Church generally recommends, since the Christian party has already left one marriage with a non-Christian.

Similarly, the Pauline Privilege may be used in polygamous cultures when one spouse receives Christian baptism. Although the newly baptized spouse is encouraged to retain the spouse to whom he or she was married first, this is not always possible. Therefore canon 1148 allows the newly baptized spouse to retain one spouse while dismissing the others. The newly Christian spouse must still provide for the needs of his or her former spouses, as well as any children born of those spouses.

Finally, the Pauline Privilege can be invoked in situations where the newly baptized spouse cannot resume cohabitation with the nonbaptized spouse due to persecution or captivity. For example, a young, nonbaptized couple attempt to flee the communist persecution in North Korea. The wife makes it to the United States, while the husband is captured and sentenced to life in a North Korean prison. Several years later the wife receives Christian baptism. Yet there is still no contact from her husband. The local ordinary may invoke the Pauline Privilege to allow this woman to contract a new marriage.

On the other hand, if the woman has strong evidence that her husband did not survive internment within a North Korean prison, but the North Korean government refuses to release a body and a death certificate was never produced, she might consider a declaration of presumed death rather than a Pauline Privilege. This process requires her to present her evidence to her pastor, who will assist her in approaching the tribunal or the diocesan bishop, depending on how the process is carried out in her diocese.

92. What is the Favor of the Faith?

Provided a marriage is not sacramental nor consummated, the Favor of the Faith may be used to dissolve a marriage. The process generally follows the same procedures as the Pauline Privilege, except that the investigation is much more intensive, as the case will ultimately be submitted to the Holy Father for dissolution. Also, in a Favor of the Faith case, the person petitioning for the favor must not be the one who is responsible for the breakdown of the marriage. The Favor of the Faith is a privilege by canon law that may be used to dissolve a marriage that is not sacramental because there is clear proof that one of the parties was never baptized. The case is submitted to the pope for dissolution (since he is the Vicar of Christ). The person asking for the favor (baptized or not) must not be the primary cause for the breakdown of the marriage. This favor can also be requested when both parties were not baptized but the baptism of only one of the parties can be proven.

When a marriage is sacramental but unconsummated, a non-consummation case must be filed, as opposed to all other types of favor cases. Perhaps a baptized couple married behind the Iron Curtain during the days of communism, and one of the spouses was captured by communist officials before the newlyweds could take up a common residence. The other spouse fled to America and several years later wishes to marry someone else.

Or perhaps two nonbaptized individuals met in a hippie commune during the sexual revolution, eloped and divorced a year later. Each spouse has since married someone else and received baptism, and one now wishes to convert to Catholicism. The Church considers the first marriage to be a valid sacrament because both spouses are now baptized. But it is unconsummated because the couple proved that they did not sleep in the same bed after receiving baptism.

In contrast, the Favor of the Faith applies when the first marriage involves only one person who was baptized at the time of marriage, or perhaps both spouses from the first marriage remain nonbaptized and neither wishes to convert. But now one of them wishes to marry a Catholic.

None of these scenarios meet all the necessary preconditions for a Pauline Privilege. However, because the previous marriage is either not sacramental or has not been consummated since becoming a sacrament, the case may proceed as either a Favor of the Faith or a non-consummation case.

93. What about a documentary process? How does this differ from the formal process?

A documentary process is one in which a marriage is invalid because of the presence of an impediment or defect of form at the time of the wedding, as proven by documents whose legitimacy is not open to question or contradiction (canon 1686). Of course, this assumes that the impediment was not dispensed by the Church when the couple attempted marriage.

Documentary process involves prior bond cases; however, the process may be used for any case involving any impediment not dispensed, as well as for defects in the canonical form of marriage.

For example, suppose a couple are handed state adoption records after their wedding. Upon opening the records they discover they are brother and sister, given up for adoption to different families shortly after birth. The couple submit to a DNA test, which subsequently proves their blood relation. The couple could then submit the records and the test results to the local tribunal under the documentary process. The adoption records and the test clearly prove the impediment of consanguinity. No formal process is needed to establish the invalidity of their marriage.

Or a man may abandon the exercise of priestly ministry, without seeking dispensation. Later he meets a Catholic woman whom he wishes to marry. He does not tell the woman about his priestly past, and he claims to be estranged from his family. She was raised Catholic and insists upon marrying in the Catholic Church. So he pretends to be a non-Christian (to avoid having to produce his baptismal certificate, which might lead to his being identified as a priest), and the couple attempt marriage after receiving a dispensation from disparity of cult. A few years later a visiting missionary recognizes the man as a former classmate from seminary. Shocked, the woman divorces the former priest. The man's baptismal certificate, when coupled with the marriage license, provide sufficient documentary proof to declare the marriage invalid. Both documents establish the man's common identity by naming the same parents, birth date, place of birth and so on.

Documentary cases do not proceed to second instance unless appealed. Both the defender of the bond and the respondent retain the right to appeal.

94. What is **ligamen,** *otherwise known as prior bond?*

For a person previously married to someone with a prior marriage, provided the Church had not dealt with the prior marriage, the documentary process may be used to prove the impediment of *ligamen*. This process is also known colloquially as *prior bond,* meaning the person or the person's former spouse was bound to a prior marriage.

In most *ligamen* cases the documentary process simply documents the prior marriage through copies of the marriage license and any baptismal certificates. However, these cases can become extremely complicated as one prior marriage invalidates another. Jacqui and Pete have found themselves dealing with over a dozen prior marriages when all the former marriages of former spouses were taken into account. For example, one party may have two prior marriages to individuals who each have two or three prior marriages of their own. Because these cases can become highly complicated, it is best to approach the tribunal with as much information as possible.

95. *What is lack of form?*

For a person who was either Catholic or married to a Catholic and did not marry according to the canonical form of marriage (in front of a Catholic priest or deacon with two witnesses), and the Catholic Church's permission was not obtained for this marriage (called a "dispensation from canonical form"), then the Church could process this case as a lack of form case. The Church calls this an administrative process. There is some dispute as to whether it is truly a documentary process, since the procedure is so simple that many dioceses permit lack of forms to be administered at the parish level without ever going through the tribunal.

The individual must prove that at least one of the former spouses was Catholic at the time of the wedding, that the couple attempted marriage outside of the Catholic form without first obtaining the proper dispensation and that the marriage is now irreparable. The individual must also establish that this marriage was never subsequently convalidated (commonly but mistakenly referred to as "blessed" by the Church—see questions 98 and 99). Most marriage tribunals accept as sufficient proof the Catholic party's baptismal record, a copy of the marriage license and the couple's divorce decree. Nevertheless, depending on particular circumstances, more evidence may be necessary.

96. What is defective form? How does it differ from lack of form?

Defective form is similar to lack of form, in that the Catholic form of marriage was not followed correctly. However, in defective form the Catholic form was followed to some degree.

Perhaps a priest presided over the wedding and there were two witnesses, but the priest lacked jurisdiction from the diocesan bishop or the parish pastor. One famous case, often shared with canon law students, involves a curial cardinal who agreed to preside over the wedding of his niece. However, he would not lower himself to request jurisdiction from the bishop of the diocese where the wedding was to be performed. The couple later divorced, and the marriage, much to the cardinal's embarrassment, was declared invalid due to defective form.

Or a case might involve a priest and no witnesses or simply one witness. Regardless, defective form may be pursued according to the documentary process if the defect is suitably documented.

97. What is canonical separation?

As an alternative to seeking a dissolution or declaration of invalidity, a person may seek canonical separation from his or her spouse. Admittedly this process has fallen into disuse in North America. However, it is still mentioned in canons 1151 to 1155.

A canonical separation, like its civil counterpart, may be used by one spouse to apply pressure to the other spouse. Traditionally this would be used when the former wishes to remain married to the latter, but the latter is engaged in behavior that is highly disruptive of the marital life.

Grounds for separation mentioned in the *Code* include adultery, unless the nonadulterous spouse directly or indirectly approved of it (canon 1152), as well as serious mental or physical abuse (canon 1153). The latter could include alcoholism if the addiction is seriously threatening the welfare of the nonalcoholic spouse or the couple's children.

The innocent spouse should seek a decree from the local ordinary. However, the innocent spouse (and children) are to leave on their own authority if delaying the departure could prove dangerous (canon 1153).

The innocent spouse can end the canonical separation at any time. However, in doing so he or she renounces the right to separate in the future unless another serious problem arises within the marriage (canon 1155).

98. I bought this book to help a family member who is going through a divorce. However, in reading it I discovered my own marriage to be invalid for lack of form. What should we do?

It is not uncommon for a couple to discover that their own marriage is invalid while helping a friend or family member through the declaration of invalidity process. Perhaps the couple eloped before a justice of the peace or married outside the Catholic Church, despite the fact that one or both parties were bound to canonical form. Or perhaps some impediment or invalidating factor comes to light. Maybe the couple entered marriage intending to exclude children but changed their minds a couple years into the marriage.

In most cases marriage enjoys the favor of the law (canon 1060). Therefore the Church continues to presume the marriage is valid. This does not apply, however, when a couple bound by canonical form married outside of the form without a proper dispensation from the Church. In cases such as this, the Church invites the couple to have a Catholic wedding ceremony.

Sometimes, the couple attempted marriage outside the Church because of an impediment to marriage. If the impediment still exists and can be dispensed, the Church will help the couple seek and obtain the proper dispensation. For example, a marriage between a baptized Catholic and a non-baptized person would require a dispensation from disparity of cult.

Upon receiving the proper dispensations, if such dispensations are needed, the couple give consent by exchanging their wedding vows according to canonical form—in other words, before a priest, deacon or other qualified officiant and two witnesses in the Western Church. The ceremony may be a public affair–some couples have elaborate church weddings–or a quiet event, depending on the needs of the couple and the discernment of the priest or deacon assisting them.

99. My wife and I eloped in Las Vegas twenty years ago. We're happily married and wish to remain so. I would like to have a Catholic wedding, but my non-Catholic wife does not understand the need to do so. What is sanatio in radice, otherwise known as "sanation"? How does this differ from having a new wedding in the Catholic Church?

For various reasons, a Catholic wedding ceremony is not always possible for couples who wish to remain married. Perhaps one of the spouses is a non-Catholic who does not understand why the Church does not recognize the couple's marriage. Or perhaps a spouse is in fragile health, and news of the invalid marriage could cause further deterioration.

Both Jacqui and Pete have come across the following scenario while giving talks on marriage to parishes: A person is exceptionally upset because his or her union is not a valid marriage, and the person's spouse is adamant that that they are married and there will be no Catholic wedding. The authors suggest the Catholic party speak to the parish priest, who can help the party apply to the bishop for a radical sanation. This solution can bring peace in the life of a torn and troubled Catholic.

Sometimes a couple wed in good faith in the Church, but their marriage is invalid because the priest made a series of mistakes while officiating. With regard to this scenario, Pete once helped with a case in which a visiting priest forgot to seek jurisdiction prior to the wedding. The oversight was discovered by the parish priest while the couple were on their honeymoon. When the couple returned, the priest approached them privately, explained the situation and entrusted them to his assistant to quietly redo the wedding. Being a newly ordained priest, however, the assistant did not realize that this ceremony also required the presence of two witnesses.

Rather than disturb the couple a second time, the pastor opted to seek *sanatio in radice,* which is a Latin expression for a "healing at the root." In other words, the marriage was made valid by the Church, at the moment of the couple's redo before the assistant pastor (although ordinarily the sanation would be retroactive to the couple's first exchange of consent).

To proceed with a sanation, the Church must first determine that both man and woman wish to persevere as a married couple. The Church must secondly be sure that the union is stable and is not likely to dissolve in the future (as much as anyone can predict such things). From here the relevant information is forwarded to the diocesan bishop and the marriage sanated.

Thus *sanatio in radice* allows the Church to validate marriages retroactively when a Church wedding is not possible, provided both parties wish to continue in the married state.

chapter nine

Concluding Thoughts on Keeping Your Marriage Together

100. Throughout this book you have shared a lot of information on why marriages break down as well as why the Church declares some marriages invalid. But what are some things couples can do to build strong and happy marriages?

While this question, strictly speaking, does not pertain to canon law, we don't mind answering it. Whether you are on your first marriage or considering a second one, there are many things you can do to strengthen your marriage. These practices are especially helpful in today's anti-family culture, in which no-fault divorce is easily sought and obtained.

So here are eight things a couple can do to strengthen their marriage.

1. Pray Together

The first thing a couple must do if they want a strong marriage is pray together. One of the biggest surprises we have encountered in tribunal work is that many couples, including those who are active in the Church (including apostolates focused specifically on pro-life and pro-family work), do not pray together as couples. When children come along, this evolves into failure to pray as a family.

A couple cannot become one in flesh unless they also strive to become one in spirit. Thus a couple should make time to pray together—not just pray, not just for each other, but together as a couple. Prayer reinforces the sacramental bond God has created between the couple. It reminds them that God stands at the center of their relationship. Additionally, it teaches them to rely upon God and trust in his providence as they face the many difficulties life throws at them.

2. Eat Together

Fast food, TV dinners, microwave meals, nutrition drinks, high-fructose corn syrup—as a society we seem to have forgotten what real food looks like. Yet nothing brings together friends and family as does a delicious home-cooked meal. Time and time again at the tribunal, Jacqui and Pete have noticed an interesting trend in the breakdown of marriages: Long before a couple stop living together, their schedule becomes so hectic that they stop eating together.

Take a good look at the Gospels. Jesus uses meals to mark important events in his life and to impart his more important teachings. For example, his first public miracle took place over a meal, the wedding feast at Cana. At the urging of our Blessed Mother, Jesus kept the meal going by changing water into wine. Thus Christ blessed the marriage by blessing the meal.

The miracle of the loaves and fishes is another good example. Having fed the multitudes, our Lord chose this moment to reveal that he is the Bread of Life, that his flesh is real food and that his blood is real drink. He revealed one of his most profound theological truths—the mystery of transubstantiation —over a meal.

Additionally, Jesus institutes the sacrament to which this truth applies most directly, the Eucharist, during the Last

Supper. Thus the Mass is modeled on the family meal, with our fellow Catholics being brothers and sisters in Christ.

3. Talk Together

"We stopped communicating." This is by far the most common answer when tribunal petitioners are asked why their marriage fell apart. Through communication spouses say, "I love you," discover each other's needs and wants and learn each other's likes and dislikes. When communication breaks down, a marriage begins to falter.

Take time to talk with your spouse, to discuss one another's hopes and frustrations, to snuggle together on the couch. At times the conversation should be serious, such as when it concerns family finances, children or unresolved differences in the relationship. Other times the conversation should be light.

For example, Jacqui and Keith love to discuss lumberjack sports and fantasy baseball. Pete and Sonya have an ongoing storyline in their marriage about the adventures of Forrest Creature, a young gopher who travels the countryside with his best friend, a sea monster, in search of bagels and cream cheese. What began as an inside joke during Pete and Sonya's courtship at university, while breakfasting together at the cafeteria, has since spawned hours of entertainment for them and their children. More importantly, the adventures of Forrest Creature allow Pete and Sonya to maintain steady communication within their marriage, so that they feel comfortable communicating with each other when serious issues arise.

4. Be Kind

On the topic of communication, engaged couples will often hear, "Communication is the key to a lasting marriage."

However, as Jacqui and Keith point out when working with engaged couples, if the "communication" is fraught with arguing, name-calling and harsh words, then it will only further destroy the relationship.

The true key to a long-lasting marriage is actually kindness. In tribunal ministry Jacqui and Pete have often seen that people treat their coworkers, friends and even complete strangers better than they treat their spouses and children. Clearly this is not the way it should be.

Sometimes the kind thing to do is to keep your mouth closed and think about being kind to your spouse. If couples remember to be kind, keep peace as the focus of their home and remember that they are called to be Christ to each other (aiding the other person to be the holiest person that he or she can be), then the marriage will be successful.

Of course, keeping the peace should never be used as an excuse to avoid discussing or addressing serious problems within the marriage. But we should approach these issues in a kind manner, respecting the dignity of one another.

5. Work With Your Differences

There's an old expression that "opposites attract," and this is often true. Jacqui and Keith were told in their prenuptial preparation, "Jacqui, you were drawn to Keith because you like to talk and he listens. Keith, you were drawn to Jacqui because you like to listen and she likes to talk."

However, couples will frequently marry hoping to change the differences in the other person instead of learning to work with the differences.

The example that Jacqui and Keith most often run across

with engaged couples is that one person is an extrovert and one is an introvert. Most of these couples have no idea how to truly communicate with each other given the differences in communication and processing styles. Extroverts tend to process information out loud and immediately. Introverts tend to need time to process information, and they do so within their own heads and within their own time frame.

Jacqui and Keith have lived this experience as a couple. Jacqui is an extrovert, and Keith is an introvert. Jacqui had to learn that Keith needed time to process information internally, and Keith had to learn that Jacqui needed to process immediately and out loud. Jacqui had to learn that though Keith was not immediately processing, he was still listening to her. Keith had to learn that he was not required to think on his feet if he did not feel he could do so.

So Jacqui now processes immediately and out loud and then gives Keith the time he needs to process. Keith regularly lets Jacqui know that he is indeed processing and will come to her soon with his opinions.

This is an example that Keith and Jacqui share with engaged couples to help them learn to work with their differences.

6. Play Together

One of the most consistent patterns in tribunal ministry is that when adultery enters a marriage, the third party is usually a coworker. Moreover, the adulterous relationship usually begins when husband and wife are spending little time together due to conflicting work schedules or serious overtime at the office.

Trust us. Whatever extra money you're bringing home from the office will seldom cover the cost of a divorce, problems with you and your children arising from the divorce and the other costs associated with a broken marriage. Learn to budget your money, and spend more time together.

The strongest marriages are those in which the couple take time to relax together, pursue common leisure activities and socialize as a couple. These activities need not be expensive. Watching a movie over pizza or going for a walk in the park is quality time and easy on the pocketbook.

7. Hold Hands

A classmate of ours, who is also a priest, happened to run into Pete and Sonya on their honeymoon. He immediately berated the young couple.

"You ought to be holding hands in public," he said, "or people won't know that you're married and love each other. Look at all those old couples down there who are still married and in love. They're holding hands."

Lack of visible affection is almost always noticeable in troubled marriages. Witnesses state that the couple never held hands, never kissed and never showed affection in public. God created us as physical beings with the capacity to feel. Quite often a hug is more reassuring to a spouse than mere words. Affection allows a couple to express physically their love for each other.

Affection should not be confused with sex. The conjugal act is a physical expression of love that should be limited to the privacy of the marital bed. Affection, on the other hand, encompasses all expressions of physical love between a married couple–including those suitable for public witness. Holding hands, hugging and kissing hello and good-bye strengthen a marriage.

8. Practice Natural Family Planning

The statistics are staggering: Couples who observe Church teaching on natural family planning (NFP) have a fraction of the divorce rate of couples who contracept. People are often shocked to discover that the divorce rate among Catholics is 50 percent; however, among couples who practice NFP, the rate drops to less than 4 percent. Among the thousands of cases Jacqui and Pete have seen in their tribunal work, only rarely have a couple seeking a declaration of invalidity or dissolution of their marriage not engaged in contraceptive practices.

Artificial birth control undermines the self-sacrifice that marriage entails, as it suppresses the natural processes within our bodies and undermines both the unitive and the procreative functions of the marital act. In short, contracepting couples never truly become one—either in spirit or in the flesh. As Pope John Paul II explains in *Familiaris Consortio*:

When couples, by means of recourse to contraception, separate [the unitive meaning and the procreative meaning] that God the Creator has inscribed in the being of man and woman and in the dynamism of their sexual communion, they act as "arbiters" of the divine plan and they "manipulate" and degrade human sexuality— and with it themselves and their married partner—by altering its value of "total" self-giving. Thus the innate language that expresses the total reciprocal self-giving of husband and wife is overlaid, through contraception, by an objectively contradictory language, namely, that of not giving oneself totally to the other. (*Familiaris Consortio*, 32)

In contrast, NFP and being open to procreation encourage marital closeness. Not only do husband and wife find themselves more open to each other's bodies and their natural processes, but they are better able to communicate with each other. There is less fear of becoming pregnant, since each spouse trusts the other to be open to the consequences of their natural relationship. Moreover, NFP requires the couple to discuss the most intimate details of their relationship—even if only to say, "According to the chart I'm fertile." This in turn encourages communication on other aspects of the couple's relationship.

For more information on NFP, contact your diocesan family life office.

We hope these eight pieces of advice will help you strengthen your marriage. And we hope you have gained some knowledge from our experiences working with marriage, declarations of invalidity and tribunals. May God bless you as you go forward from here.

notes

Chapter Four: Impediments to Marriage

1. One can leave the Church through a "formal act" by contacting the bishop of the diocese in which the person was baptized, in writing. Usually this involves the person stating that he or she is leaving the Church to become an atheist or an adherent to another religious sect. Merely ceasing to practice the Catholic faith actively or joining another faith tradition is not sufficient to leave the Church.

   It is important to note that this formal defection affects only marriage. All other areas of Church law still apply to a person who has formally defected from the Church.

Chapter Eight: Other Options

1. This book also features Pete's story of his return to the Catholic faith and his decision to become a canon lawyer.

ABOUT THE AUTHORS

PETE VERE, J.C.L., is a canon lawyer, author, journalist and professor of canon law and catechesis. He writes for a number of Catholic and secular publications, works as an independent canonical consultant for several dioceses and teaches at Catholic Distance University. He obtained his license in canon law from Saint Paul University in Ottawa, Canada. He is coauthor, with Michael Trueman, of *Surprised by Canon Law: 150 Questions Catholics Ask About Canon Law* (volumes 1 and 2). Pete, his wife, Sonya, and their four children live in Sault Ste. Marie, Canada.

JACQUI RAPP, J.D., J.C.L., is a wife, mother and canon lawyer. She is currently an independent canonical consultant and is an Assessor, Judge and Defender of the Bond for several U.S. dioceses. Author of numerous articles in both print and online magazines, she gives talks on marriage and nullity, and works with engaged couples in her parish. Jacqui, with her husband, Keith, and their daughters, Alexandra and Sabina, are members of the Catholic Community of St. Francis of Assisi in Louisville, Kentucky.